THE
GRIEF AND
Happiness
HANDBOOK

A Supportive Guide To Help You Reclaim
Your Life While Grieving

The Grief and Happiness Handbook
Copyright © Emily Thiroux Threatt

Published and printed by Ignite Publishing, a division of JBO Global Inc.
5569-47th Street Red Deer, AB
Canada, T4N1S1 1-877-677-6115

Cover design by Sinisa Poznanovic and Katie Smetherman
Book design by JB Owen, Katie Smetherman, and Kristine Joy Magno
Edited by JB Owen, Mimi Safiyah, and Zoe Wong.
Designed in Canda, Printed in China
ISBN: 979-8-9872121-4-1
First edition: July, 2023

Ordering Information: Quantity sales. Special discounts are available on quantity purchases by corporations, associations, and others. For details, contact the publisher at the above address. Programs, products, or services provided by the author are found by contacting them directly. Resources named in the book are found in the resources pages at the back of the book.

Author Details: Available in the author bio section at the back of the book.

THE GRIEF AND *Happiness* HANDBOOK

A Supportive Guide To Help You Reclaim
Your Life While Grieving

EMILY THIROUX THREATT

Founder of the Grief and Happiness Alliance
International Best-selling Author

Published by *I*gnite Publishing, a division of JBO Global Inc.
IGNITEYOU.LIFE

DEDICATION

To Rev. Rachel Hollander, Patti Ross, Rose Rabinov, Sydney Thiroux, Judy Kirkpatrick, and Rev. Richard Carlini—the Board of the *Grief and Happiness Alliance Nonprofit Organization*, for their unconditional love and support.

To Rev. Joanna Thompson Gabriel, October 8, 1945 - September 21, 2021, who inspired and fully supported the development of the *Grief and Happiness Alliance* concept.

TESTIMONIALS

Emily Thiroux Threatt has written what I consider a really important book and one of the most profoundly helpful books I have read on Grief. The book is practical with things people can do to help them deal with grief and loss.

JACK CANFIELD
FOUNDER OF THE *CHICKEN SOUP FOR THE SOUL®* SERIES
AND AN AWARD-WINNING SPEAKER AND INTERNATIONALLY
RECOGNIZED LEADER IN PERSONAL DEVELOPMENT.

The Grief and Happiness Handbook is brilliant work by Emily Thiroux Threatt, who writes from the heart and shoots straight from the hip to deliver the way to live a more awakened life. She charts the course for how to walk through the shadows of grief into the light. With Emily as your guide, you are in good hands.

RICKIE BYARS
ACCLAIMED SINGER-SONGWRITER IN THE INSPIRATIONAL/
NEW THOUGHT MUSIC GENRE AND A SOCIAL ACTIVIST.

In this beautiful and profound *Grief and Happiness Handbook*, Emily Thiroux Threatt shows how grief is a natural and essential process when we've experienced loss. It's not something that can or should be bypassed, but we can experience it without losing our inner well-being. She offers clear and brilliant guidance about how to grieve with greater grace and peace while also honoring your feelings and the life of the loved one you've lost. This is a life-changing concept.

MARCI SHIMOFF
#1 NEW YORK TIMES BEST-SELLING AUTHOR OF *HAPPY FOR
NO REASON, LOVE FOR NO REASON*, AND CO-AUTHOR OF SIX
CHICKEN SOUP FOR THE SOUL SERIES TITLES.

As the tears of grief fill your eyes, Emily Thiroux Threatt serves you *The Grief and Happiness Handbook*—a treasured heart-centered home for your tears to land on the pages. Your understanding, empathy, creativity, autonomy, and safety needs are met with hope, healing, and happiness.

DR. VALERIE SIMONSEN

The gift of Emily's work is useful, practical, authentic, and healing. We all deal with grief. Having a way to navigate it through writing and self-discovery allows us to experience more light on our journey.

REVEREND RACHEL HOLLANDER

Emily's words are not only powerful, but they are also raw, truthful, and inspiring. As someone who has experienced profound loss and grief, she can speak those truths in a way that will touch your heart while leaving you feeling inspired that hope and happiness are possible once more.

JOHN POLO
COACH, AUTHOR, AND SPEAKER

Carrying on in the face of grief and reclaiming your joy—what a concept! And it is possible when you use Emily Thiroux Threatt's work as your guide. From practice prompts, sharing stories of her losses, and finding joy again, I find it very useful as a grief professional. I've participated in her journaling workshops and attended the Grief and Happiness Alliance—amazing work manifested by the gifted Emily.

REV. RICHARD CARLINI
RN BA C-RNPCMINISTER AT THE
UNITY CENTER OF DAVIS

Emily blends the gentle spirit of aloha with concrete tools that provide comfort and transformation, allowing grievers to integrate sorrow and happiness into their unique healing experience.

SARA J. COBB
FOUNDER, MYGRIEFCONNECTION.ORG

CONTENTS

Foreword

by Marci Shimoff

As surprising as it sounds, you can be happy and grieve simultaneously. While our society doesn't teach that, there is a way to have a state of inner peace and well-being that doesn't depend on our circumstances—I call that being "happy for no reason."

In this beautiful and profound *Grief and Happiness Handbook*, Emily Thiroux Threatt details how grief is a natural and important process when we've experienced loss. It's not something that can or should be bypassed, but we can experience it without losing our inner well-being. She goes on to offer clear and brilliant guidance about how you can grieve with greater grace and peace while also honoring your own feelings of grief and the life of the loved one you've lost.

That's a life-changing concept.

I'd always wanted to experience lasting and unshakeable happiness, even amid the most challenging situations, and so I did extensive study in the field of happiness, searching for answers. I spoke with top researchers and experts in the field and interviewed 100 of the happiest people in the world to learn their secrets. I tried out what they were doing, and it worked! These discoveries became the basis for my book, *Happy for No Reason*.

A few years after the book was published, my father and mother, both of whom I was very close with, passed away. After spending most of my life in utter fear of losing them, I was amazed to experience a deep sense of peace alongside my grief. I felt so fortunate to embrace the natural process of grieving in a way that made the journey very rich. I experienced firsthand how grief and happiness can go side by side.

More than a decade ago, I began training other people to teach what I'd learned about happiness so they could share it in their work. I'm thrilled that Emily, the author of this book, is one of my star graduates. She became certified as a *Happy For No Reason* Trainer so she could help people move through their grieving process.

Emily now uses happiness practices to complement how she guides people in dealing with grief. And the results speak for themselves. Her clients and students are finding deeper peace and well-being amidst their loss. Emily's important work continues to grow through The Grief and Happiness Alliance, a weekly online gathering offering tools, practices, and community connection for people grieving around the world.

The *Grief and Happiness Handbook* is a great follow-up to the wisdom and tools Emily shared in her book, *Loving and Living Your Way Through Grief*. Both of these books are a gift to anyone facing grief or loss.

I know that no matter your specific situation, you'll find what's shared in this handbook to be extraordinarily helpful. Find a cozy place to curl up with this book and discover the comfort, support, love, and happiness waiting for you on every page. My heart and my love are with you in your grief.

–Marci Shimoff, #1 *New York Times* best-selling author of *Happy for No Reason* and *Love for No Reason*, and co-author of six titles in the *Chicken Soup for the Soul* series.

PREFACE

This book is being shared with you in the spirit of creating more happiness and joy on the planet despite the grieving many of us are dealing with. I have had two husbands die; both had congestive heart failure and renal failure that led to dialysis. Though I have dealt with the grief of many losses in my life, my husbands were the hardest for me. I felt very much alone when Jacques died in 2006 after 22 years together. My wonderful friend Yvonne stayed with me for months before he died and a few months after, which helped with the transition, but when she was gone, I didn't know what to do.

Ron and I spent ten years together after Jacques had passed and I worked through my grief to once again find happiness. Our relationship was always lived in the moment, and though we knew during the last couple of years that his body was winding down, we focused fully on living. When he was gone, I was very lonely. I turned to reading books about grief, seeking comfort and guidance on what to do next, but most of the books I found were memoirs. While the stories were interesting, I wasn't gaining the help I was seeking to guide me.

Ron's dear friend Chappy died seven months after Ron did. They were very close. Chappy even called Ron Dad since he was so much younger. He died without warning one evening, and when I heard, my first thought was of his wife, Lori. At her age, I doubt they had considered either of them dying, and with teenage daughters at home, I was concerned that she would feel lost and unsure of what to do. I knew that she would be surrounded by people telling her what would be best for her, so I wrote her a letter with suggestions on what she did need to do and what she didn't need to do based on my experience.

My first suggestion was for her to take good care of herself and trust her own pace in the grieving process.

After Chappy's celebration of life was over, Lori let me know how much my letter had helped. That made me realize I could do more. Since we were living an ocean apart, I decided to write to her each week with thoughts and suggestions that would help her along the way during that first year of loss. I crafted fifty-two cards with pictures I had taken on the island of Maui, where I live. I included a special message in each one. My hope was that those messages would be supportive of her in finding the happiness she deserved.

When I wrote the 52 weeks of messages, I knew I could use those to write the book that I had been seeking during my grieving. I soon discovered that I had an outline for a book with fifty-two chapters! That's a lot of chapters for a book! I realized a book that long would most likely be overwhelming, so I divided the chapters into two books, creating a nice balance of content between them. The first book, *Loving and Living Your Way Through Grief,* was published at the beginning of 2021, and this book came to market in 2023.

In these past few years, I created the *Grief and Happiness Alliance,* which hosts weekly online meetings for those dealing with grief and loss where we write about different topics each week concerning grief and/or happiness, then we share our writing. This has led to comfort, support, and friendships for those participating. Because I didn't want people to pay to attend this group, I invited friends to create a nonprofit organization to cover the group's expenses. They encouraged me to add more workbook exercises in this second book to give the readers even more guidance; thus, *The Grief and Happiness Handbook* was created. And, a stunning box set of grief and happiness cards has also been created from the 52 weeks of suggestions, including the wonderful photos I took.

All profits from the sales of the handbook and the card deck go to support the work of the *Grief and Happiness Nonprofit Organization* so that we are able to provide even more comfort and support to more people around the world. These products are meant not only for the people dealing with grief and loss themselves but also for the loved ones of those grieving, helping them see ways they can support their loved ones.

We all deal with grief and loss at different times throughout our lives. And we can all provide comfort and support to each other along the way. Reading this book can help support and comfort you in this pursuit. It has been my honor to write such a treasured collection of suggestions and support during such an important time in the lives of those suffering from loss. My wish is that you use this book, either for yourself or by sharing it with someone in need so that it brings more happiness and joy to everyone who reads it.

INTRODUCTION

Let me start off by saying welcome, congratulations, and thank you. You are about to begin the next steps in your grieving process, which I promise will be both healing and comforting. Congratulations on caring about yourself enough to take these steps to find your happiness. I appreciate you for allowing me to be the one to assist you in getting to where it is you desire to be.

I want you to know that everything can only get better from here. You have the ability to define your future and make the choices you need. I want to be someone you can lean on and trust, and one who will help you through this journey by making everything you are going through a little bit smoother. My goal is that together we will begin the process of awakening to how your life is changing and then take action to set new intentions that will allow you to emerge more clear about the life you are creating on the other side.

I have dealt with many losses in my life over the years, from losing two husbands to losing my parents, sister, and many friends. I have come through my losses with a realization that my life's purpose is to give love and offer comfort to those who are also experiencing loss in their lives. In dealing with my grief, I found that writing about how I was feeling helped me find joy and showed me how I could bring hope to others to help them find joy, also. Those experiences have led me to become a guide for those who need support on their journey as they start to feel open to loving and living again.

I discovered my gift was helping people deal with loss and grief, and that led me to write my first book, *Loving and Living Your Way Through Grief*. After I finished that book, I realized I had so much more to share. I wanted to continue the healing process, so I could help people further discover ways they could move forward to plan and experience a strong and happy life. That led to this book, *The Grief and Happiness Handbook: Taking Action to Thrive Through Grief.* When we experience loss of any kind, the early days and months can go by in a blur. Many times the things we have to do and the tasks we need to perform are too difficult to deal with. Yet as the days, then months, pass, we find ourselves in a different emotional place. The questions that roll through our minds now are, *How do I carry on? What do I do now? How can I move through grief and find happiness?*

Although your life is before you, taking those first steps into the unknown can be challenging. As you make your way through this book, you will explore how you would like your life to progress and what new things you can try along the way. Discovering how to incorporate happiness back into your life will give you a beautiful new perspective as you move forward. You can actively plan your 'new life' and find new ways of being that support you intrinsically.

Grief and happiness can co-exist. There is a whole tribe of individuals around the world who find themselves in a place of sorrow that no one asks for or wants to be, yet through it, they find the ability to reclaim their happiness. By approaching the process with an open heart and open arms, you can learn to love, share, feel, open, and discover the best version of yourself that you deserve to be.

I am here to encourage you on your way. Take my hand... we've got this.

HOW THIS BOOK CAN HELP YOU

Whatever your circumstance may be, this book offers you resourceful support and helpful practices through tips, strategies, and ideas, along with personal stories of individuals going through grief like you. It is written to encourage you to step forward in a positive way and discover how life is going to be as you proceed. Each chapter contains ways for you to look at your life from a new perspective and has practices that will help put what you are learning into action. Throughout the chapters, you will find personal stories designed to give you caring perspectives from fellow grievers. Reading their stories will help you understand you are not alone in the experiences you are having. By sharing these real-life stories, I hope you will discover new ways to foster joy in living once again. You can move from feeling stuck and alone to feeling optimistic and supported as you enter a new experience of who you can become.

As you read the book from start to finish, use it like a Handbook where you pick and choose a topic that pertains to an issue that most needs your attention. Wherever you are in the process of grief, or if you have been living with it for years, within these pages you will find inspiration to support you, along with practices to comfort you on your healing journey. I encourage you to do the practices that most resonate with you and will enable you to feel supported as you actively seek a new way of being in the world. Let each chapter stimulate and encourage you to use the tools you need to establish the new life you are ready to enjoy.

My goal is that as you go through the many suggestions included here, you will be motivated to move forward, using the grief you feel for your loved ones to inspire you to become the person you are meant to be. I want you to always remember I am here for you and will be with you every step of the way. I know firsthand the grieving process and believe if we do it together, you will come out stronger on the other side.

HOW TO USE THIS BOOK

Inside this book, you will find suggestions and practical actions for you to use to reclaim your joy and find your happiness. You will also find suggested practices and key takeaways from each chapter as a summary. The exercises throughout the chapters are designed to guide you in harnessing your strength and utilizing your inner knowledge to make the best choices moving forward. They are written with love and care to ensure you are in charge of your present life and future needs. The practices are there to get you moving and doing things for your emotional and physical well-being that has your mind thinking and your body taking action. The practices are vital parts of moving you toward the future you desire. As a way of helping you process all the new learning, a summary of the key points from the chapter are at the end for quick reference and a constant reminder of what you have learned.

Each chapter includes stories from my personal experience and the experiences of others in my extended community who have also journeyed loss and found a way to reclaim their joy. I included these stories not only to help ease your journey but also to assist you in moving through the feelings of isolation and loneliness. These relatable stories will help you to know that others who have been where you are were able to come out of their grief and eventually feel renewed.

You can benefit your personal progress by choosing to use this book in a way that will help you to attain more comfort and strength. You may review the table of contents and begin with a particular chapter and practice that calls to you. Or, follow each chapter sequentially and practice the suggestions week by week. Alternatively, you may choose to read and follow the chapters daily and only use some of the suggested practices in a continuous or repetitive style. However you choose to engage with this book is up to you, and it's all okay; it will be the perfect and right path for you.

You may want to incorporate the suggested practices into your daily routine. For example, before my husband Ron and I moved to Maui, we started each day by reading something inspirational, meditating, and praying together. Continuing that practice on Maui, we invited our new *Ohana* (Hawaiian word for family) to join us. That daily practice grounded us, ensuring we started each day positively. Additionally, I developed my own daily practice of writing a list of things I am grateful for, which I still use today. That daily devoted practice strengthens me and brings me joy despite my losses.

I encourage you to *take your time* as you move through this book. There are various practices, some of which may be familiar to you, and while may be new. Activities such as journaling, gratitude, meditation, prayer, setting intentions, saying affirmations, and more, are all designed to help you through the process in new and unique ways. Feel free to try everything at least once and do more of what works best for you. Your body and brain need new stimulation to create new thoughts and memories.

Throughout this entire process, you will learn that there is no 'one-size-fits-all' timeline for experiencing loss. Each person's experience is their own. The important thing is to remember that you are whole, complete, and perfect no matter where you are in your journey. You will discover that using these practices will help you find peace, comfort, and love as you continue to carry on.

FOUR TIPS ON USING THIS BOOK

1. Take your time reading the book. Pace yourself by not reading more than one chapter at a time.
2. Use a highlighter when you read. Mark what you want to remember and come back to review again.
3. Do the practices at the end of each chapter that most resonate for you.
4. Complete the *Happiness Habits* at the end of each chapter and integrate them into your life.
5. Take care of yourself at all times. Use this book as a way of giving yourself loving support.

HOW TO CREATE HAPPINESS HABITS AND GOOD PRACTICES

Habits are those things we do all the time. A habit can be helpful if it is positive, but it can also be hurtful if it stops us from being our best selves. Habits can be tricky since we do them all the time. They can sneak up on us and become a common occurrence before we even know it, or they can be something we've done for so long that we don't realize the outcome it creates. A good habit can push us toward where we want to be. A not-so-good habit can keep us from ever reaching where it is we want to get to.

When you deal with grief and loss, you face major changes that affect your ability to create helpful new habits and recognize the habits that may be holding you back. Creating and embracing new habits is one of the best ways to provide invaluable support along your journey through grief, so I have created a section for you to focus on exactly that.

Each chapter throughout the book is designed to help you form effective habits that will support you in creating actions that will help you heal. The *Happiness Habits* section at the end of each chapter is designed to incorporate new habits into your daily practice so that you will feel the comfort, support, and love that valuable habits can instill. Each Happiness Habits section comprises four parts; *Your Intention, Your Gratitude, Your Happiness,* and *Your Affirmation.* Take the time to write out your response in each of the four areas for every chapter. Write your responses directly in the book or in a separate journal you use for your thoughts and responses to this work.

Doing this process is an important step in your healing journey as it sets you up for success in many areas of your life. To know how to be effective, read the examples below to understand how you can complete the sections when you come across them going forward.

YOUR INTENTION

An intention is what you intend to do. Writing intentions is not writing a 'To Do' list or a goal of *what* to do. Writing intentions is *how* you intend to be going forward and *who* you want to become. For instance, *what kind of a person do you want to be? What do you commit to? What is your focus?*
Examples of writing intentions:
 * I am kind and caring in all I do.
 * I practice integrity in all I do.
 * I focus on being positive in all I do.

YOUR GRATITUDE

Practicing gratitude is one of the most powerful and easiest practices you can do to enhance the joy and positive energy in your life. Jack Canfield suggests that to amplify your gratitude when you write it out always start with the words "I am happy and grateful that (or for)........" For example:

* I am happy and grateful that I write in my journal daily, which brings me self-comfort and support.
* I am happy and grateful for my loving circle of friends.
* I am happy and grateful that my dog runs to greet me each time I come home.

YOUR HAPPINESS

The practice of writing about your happiness reminds you regularly of the importance of experiencing happiness in your life even while you are grieving. After you read each chapter, write what about that chapter brought you happiness or how you can use what you learned to bring more happiness into your life. For instance:

* In the chapter about changing your surroundings, you could write about how painting your bedroom a color you love will remind you of that happiness each time you enter the room.
* In the chapter about putting your affairs in order, you will realize the comfort of knowing what important documents you need to have up to date for when the need arises.
* In the chapter about how laughter is the best medicine, you learn to allow yourself to enjoy the positive things you experience.

YOUR AFFIRMATION

According to *Psychology Today,* affirmations work because they have the ability to program our minds into believing the stated concept. Positive Affirmations can also help to reduce stress levels and increase happiness endorphins.[1] To write an affirmation, decide what you want to change and why you want that change, then write it out, starting your statement with "I" and using the present tense.

---

[1] (https://www.psychologytoday.com/us/blog/the-wise-open-mind/201108/5-steps-make-affirmations-work-you).

For instance:

* I make the best decisions for my happiness.
* I am strong and healthy.
* I am always creating my beautiful life by practicing unconditional love.

You've come this far, so I encourage you to take the time to do the Happiness Habits along with the suggested Practices, Key Points, and Action lists throughout the book. There's a quote by JB Owen that says, "The hardest step is taking the first step.[2]" Having this book in your hand is the first step, and you've accomplished that. The next step is for you to start the healing process to find the joy and happiness you deserve today, tomorrow, and all the days to come.

Use this book in all possible ways to move you from feeling stuck to feeling liberated, from feeling lost to finding yourself again. Let it answer your questions and guide you on your way toward a greater version of yourself. Know that I am here for you every step of the way. I sincerely wish that you find love, support, joy, peace, inspiration, comfort, and the desire to savor each moment and live in peace and harmony.

It's time to get started. Let's find some joy and happiness.

---

[2] Lady JB Owen https://jbowen.website/

CHAPTER 1
HAPPINESS AND GRIEF

"I don't think of all the misery, but of all the beauty that remains."
—ANNE FRANK

I was married to Jacques Thiroux for 22 years. He was a brilliant philosophy professor and bioethicist. He also loved to sing and act, especially in comedies. Our life together was filled with joy and laughter, and Jacques laughed often. We had a beautiful, peach-faced cockatiel that we tried to teach to talk, but he refused. However, he did figure out how to laugh in Jacques' voice. When Jacques laughed, the bird laughed. The bird laughed when he heard laughter on television, and sometimes he laughed to entertain himself. We couldn't help but laugh along. With all the laughter in my life, I couldn't help but be happy.

After Jacques died, I found it difficult to do anything. I didn't smile for months. The grief was overwhelming. I ran across Mari Shimoff's book, *Happy for No Reason*, and decided to read it because I had no reason to be happy. I am grateful her book spoke to me. I read about other people's challenges and saw that they could find happiness. In that book, I found hope that I, too, would be able to be happy once again.

The more I focused on happiness, the more joy I had in my life. A few years later, I met Reverend Ron Threatt and found even more to be joyful for. As I became more mindful, I welcomed more and more happiness. Ron and I had ten wonderful years together; then he passed away. Having experienced the depths of despair after Jacques' death, I knew I didn't want to fall into such sorrow again. I embraced my passion for writing and turned to my journal for comfort and support. The more I wrote, the better I felt. I paid attention to the things I was writing about that helped me the most and continued exploring my life in that direction. Then it dawned on me that if the kind of writing I was doing was helping me so much, I could teach others who were experiencing the loss of a loved one to write in ways that would help them also.

I started inviting people into my home to write with me once a month. We became a loving support group where we would write and discuss what we wrote. We decided we wanted to be together more, so we started gathering every other week. We learned from each other's experiences and gained comfort from each other's healing. We shared so much love in that group. Then the pandemic hit. While many ventures immediately went online, the people in our group found they wanted personal contact by gathering instead of in front of a computer. Due to sheltering-in that group faded away.

I missed my writing companions and wanted to support those who were grieving, so I decided to begin again by hosting a writing group online. People joined from around the country, and I was back in the swing of fulfilling my purpose; helping others through their grief. Then, a dear friend of my husband died suddenly. He and his wife were close friends and much younger than we were. I was so concerned for her that I started writing her cards every week with words of support and things that could help her during the first year without her husband. As I looked at the cards I was writing, I realized I had an outline for a book. That was the catalyst for my first grief book, *Loving and Living Your Way Through Grief*. I loved writing and working on the message of living through your grief to help even more people who were hurting. Despite all I was doing to support my growing community, I felt something inside of me was still missing.

When I was looking for a book to read to help me deal with my grief, I found Marci Shimoff's book *Happy for No Reason*. I remembered seeing Marci in the movie *The Secret* and liking what she said, so I read her book, which wasn't about grief but did help me feel better. Then I noticed online a *Happy For No Reason* Certified Trainer Program, and it dawned on me that happiness was what I needed to focus on. I looked through my copy of *Happy For No Reason* and knew instinctively I belonged in the program. I loved being surrounded by all the happiness we experienced while learning valuable, realigning lessons.

I discovered what was missing from all the work I was doing with grief: happiness. That realization immediately changed my life.

Once I completed my training, I was inspired to create the *Grief and Happiness* podcast knowing the more I shared about how people can grieve and be happy at the same time, the more happiness I could bring into the world. I hosted guests from all over the world who have suffered from a loss and discovered ways to be happy while grieving. I wanted to normalize the concept of being happy while grieving by demonstrating how it could be done. My guests had so many different inspirational messages, from writing books to creating beautiful public memorials, to becoming art therapists, to creating support groups, and more. Despite all the good I was doing, I knew I wanted to do more.

I was inspired to create an online peer support group encouraging those attending to write together, share their stories, and learn from my training in happiness practices. While I loved the idea, I quickly discovered that when grief and happiness are mentioned in the same sentence, people react with either confusion or the opinion that using those words together was an 'oxymoron and seemly contradictory.' I decided to prove them wrong; happiness and grief *could* go hand in hand.

At first, I researched if others agreed with my 'out of the ordinary' topic. I discovered that other people were simultaneously writing about experiencing grief and happiness, which allowed me to see that I was on the right track. It is part of the human condition to experience conflicting emotions at the same time. We can feel frustrated at our friends for being late to dinner, and at the same time, we can smile with happiness when they come through the door with a big hello and a hug, saying how happy we are they arrived. Or, a person can be sad when they don't get the job they wanted, yet happy when that disappointment made way for a better position. There are no rules about what you are allowed to feel or experience when you are mourning, so there should also not be rules regarding what you need to experience to get through the grieving process.

Amazingly, our bodies naturally find ways to balance our emotions; oxymorons don't apply. Many people get to a place where they feel stuck in their grief because they don't know what they can do to change how they are feeling or find a way to move forward. The good news is we can get relief from grief by allowing ourselves to go with our emotions' natural ebb and flow. As raw, sharp, and overwhelming as initial grief can be, your body will strive to adjust because it is unhealthy and somewhat impossible to stay at the peak of pain for a long period of time. It is natural to seek comfort in the grieving process, to feel better, and smile again. Smiling is such an important part of life. You crave smiling because smiling produces endorphins and lowers blood pressure; smiling is contagious and can lead to smiles being reflected back to you. All of this information proved to me that teaching happiness was needed more than ever.

Happiness may gradually seep into your life without you noticing. One day you realize you are naturally smiling when you see a new baby or are enjoying a piece of chocolate cake. When we get out of our own way by releasing the feelings of guilt that cause us to think we can't be happy while grieving, we can move forward and gradually welcome back the joys in life.

Coming to terms with grief and allowing tears and sadness to help you move through the process will be the starting point in your journey forward. You can do this process independently, but eventually, you will crave the company of people who relate to what you are experiencing without judgment and can add needed support. Those closest to you may be dealing with their own grief and, therefore, may find it hard to support you in your loss. Finding a safe space where others are on the same journey as you can be a great aid in your healing and a profound gift.

I decided to create a pilot program by inviting a broad spectrum of those experienced in the field of grief to join me in the process of what I thought a beneficial healing program would be. I called it the *Grief and Happiness Alliance* because it represented a group of people who've come together to support each other in moving through their grief. We brainstormed ideas, and then I facilitated a session on what a group meeting would be like for those needing help. We recapped after the session, and there was overwhelming support for the concept. One of our group members, Rev. Joanna Thompson Gabriel, said, "This is an idea whose time has come."

Buoyed by that enthusiasm, I shared that my challenge with the idea was that I wasn't comfortable charging people for peer support to help them deal with grief. So, the group suggested they form a nonprofit organization that would cover the expenses and shows the people who attend the meetings the value of our support network. We then formed the *Grief and Happiness Alliance Nonprofit Organization* with the intention of reaching even more people with the message of being able to grieve and be happy at the same time. Our idea led to this book, *The Grief and Happiness Handbook*.

I share this story with you because I feel if you know the origins of this work, it will help you see that I am like you and the team behind this mission have all gone through the sorrow you are going through now. We have all felt grief tugging at our souls and yet found solace and comfort in working together to make happiness more prevalent than grief. We are excited that you are here and know that your work is some of the hardest work a person can do but the most rewarding when done in community.

LESSONS FROM THE GRIEF AND HAPPINESS ALLIANCE

What is often missing when people are dealing with grief is companionship and having someone to talk to who understands what they are going through. Often, when people do get together, they aren't sure what to talk about for fear of triggering painful memories or tears. Knowing how much comfort can come from sharing, the Alliance encouraged writing so that individuals could find their voice without having to share in person. Writing is a cathartic healing process that enables individuals to express much-needed emotions in a safe and secure way. Writing together allows us to explore our thoughts and feelings comfortingly. Stimulating ideas to write about and having someone to listen to what we share helps us to open up to what we are experiencing and know that we aren't alone.

Throughout this book, you will find many writing practices designed to support you in moving through your grief. Some of them include writing about a different topic each week, like finding happiness by doing what you love or writing a list of your ten favorite things and writing *why* they make you happy. Writing is a huge part of finding happiness, and I want to start things off by encouraging you to write in your journal as you simultaneously work through this book. Each time you write, you process more and more. That process will help you find your joy and the strength to move forward in your life. It may not sound easy at this precise moment, but the entire Alliance guarantees that over time, positive feelings will arrive!

Let's start by writing out a list of the happiness practices you can implement. To make it easier, I've made a list to help you get started and encourage you to use any of mine to add to yours. Taking action is required to move from where we are to a new emotional place. Here are some actions to try that can help you incorporate happiness into your life while grieving. You can do them anytime. You can even start right now.

CREATE YOUR OWN HAPPINESS PRACTICE

Having your own personal practice will remind you regularly that your happiness is already within you. You can do any of the things on the list whenever you want to. Tailor what you practice to suit your needs.

1. When you first wake up in the morning, smile, stretch, and say hello to a beautiful day before you do anything else.
2. Drink a full glass of water when you first get up to show love to your body, thanking it for supporting you.
3. Practice great hygiene. There is nothing more refreshing than a morning shower.
4. Brush your teeth. When grieving, it's often easy to let self-care slide, which doesn't help you feel good. Give your teeth the love they need.
5. Eat a nourishing breakfast, skipping processed foods and sugary treats.
6. Plan your day to include breaks and eliminate pressure. Jamming too many things to do in a day builds stress.
7. Include human interaction in your day that isn't work-related. Go for a walk with a friend or join someone for coffee.
8. Don't do anything you don't want to do.
9. Do something you enjoy.

10. *Try something new, anything from a different flavor drink to going to a gallery you haven't been to, to listening to music or attending an art class.*

11. Spend time with someone older than you to seek wisdom and solace in their stories.

12. Spend some time with someone younger than you. You can learn so much about enjoying life and living in the moment.

13. Set a timer to remind you to smile every hour.

14. Read something you want to learn about or enjoy.

15. Give something away to someone who will appreciate it.

16. Volunteer to help a cause you believe in.

17. Text or call a friend who would love to hear from you.

18. Eat something you haven't tried before.

19. Write in your journal.

20. Remember something that brought you joy. *What can you do to have more of that joy?*

Notice that all the list items have no requirement to focus on grief. The point here is to be happy. Being happy can help you live longer and be healthier; the more focused you are on happiness, the happier you will be. I wrote the list based on the happiness practice I created for myself. At first, I would look through my list and choose things to do, but I discovered the longer I used the list, I wasn't having to refer back to it because I found myself easily incorporating these happiness practices into my life. I even began to add new things that I could do bring me happiness as time progressed.

PRACTICE: CREATE YOUR OWN HAPPINESS PRACTICE

It's your turn to write your list.

Start small, incorporate some of my suggestions, and gently ask yourself what things make you happy that you can do each day to move in the direction of feeling happier. Using some of the things from my list to remind you of things you can do to help yourself be happy, choose at least one thing to focus on and do it today. I'm sure there are lots of things that would help you be happy that I wouldn't think of, so be creative in creating your own special list.

What do you need to do differently to incorporate happiness into your life?
Keep track in your journal or in the space provided here of what works best for you and what you can shift so that happiness is more accessible to you. Keep adding to the list of things you would love to do that would bring you happiness. Start one by one by doing each thing you wrote down. The more you focus on happiness, the less time you will need or want to spend mourning. And that's a good thing. Enjoy!

KEY TIPS FROM CHAPTER ONE

* Give yourself permission to grieve and be happy simultaneously.
* Create your own happiness action list.
* Share your grief with others who are also grieving.
* Be free and ease into your joy-filled life.

TAKE ACTION

HAPPINESS HABITS
Your Intention
* Write an *Intention* about how you incorporate grief and happiness into your life.

I intend to ⎯⎯⎯⎯⎯⎯⎯⎯⎯⎯⎯⎯⎯⎯⎯⎯⎯⎯⎯⎯⎯⎯⎯⎯

⎯⎯⎯⎯⎯⎯⎯⎯⎯⎯⎯⎯⎯⎯⎯⎯⎯⎯⎯⎯⎯⎯⎯⎯⎯⎯⎯⎯⎯⎯⎯⎯⎯⎯⎯

⎯⎯⎯⎯⎯⎯⎯⎯⎯⎯⎯⎯⎯⎯⎯⎯⎯⎯⎯⎯⎯⎯⎯⎯⎯⎯⎯⎯⎯⎯⎯⎯⎯⎯⎯

⎯⎯⎯⎯⎯⎯⎯⎯⎯⎯⎯⎯⎯⎯⎯⎯⎯⎯⎯⎯⎯⎯⎯⎯⎯⎯⎯⎯⎯⎯⎯⎯⎯⎯⎯

⎯⎯⎯⎯⎯⎯⎯⎯⎯⎯⎯⎯⎯⎯⎯⎯⎯⎯⎯⎯⎯⎯⎯⎯⎯⎯⎯⎯⎯⎯⎯⎯⎯⎯⎯

Your Gratitude

    * Write what you are *grateful* for about learning new ways to focus on happiness.

I am happy and grateful that _____

_____

_____

_____

_____

_____

Your Happiness

    * What have you *dreamed* of that you know would make you happy? Create a plan to get started making that happen.

_____

_____

_____

_____

_____

Your Affirmation

    * Write a positive *affirmation* stating when you are the happiest.

_____

_____

_____

_____

_____

*

CHAPTER 2
YOUR TRANSFORMATION TIMELINE

"I am so grateful for the rhythm of the universe that is everything."
–REV. GRETA SESHETA

G rief often seemed as though it would be never-ending for me, especially after I had two husbands pass away. Days seemed to stand still, and nights were even longer. I was living alone and spent much time lying in bed. Eventually, I turned the television on and discovered Hallmark™ Christmas movies. They worked for me because the plot was basically the same, so it didn't matter if I fell asleep and missed the full story; nobody died in them.

Eventually, I started waking up and craved fresh air, so I went outside, and my mind started to wander. That was when I picked up a notebook and started writing the random thoughts floating through my mind. As my thoughts started coalescing, I wondered what was next for me. I wrote about what I wanted to be, to have, to do. The more I wrote, the more sense I made, and I realized I needed to wake up, pay attention, and start moving forward in my life.

I know your grief. I acknowledge your pain. Don't let anyone tell you to move more quickly through it. Only you know how much time you need to spend on it. There is no shame or blame involved in your experience. Spend all the time you need coming to understand your grief. Know that it's okay not to feel it every moment. You can cry. You can sit quietly. You can smile. You can experience joy. Your timeline is your own.

I was shocked one day when a friend of mine told me his employer spoke harshly to him after he returned from the three-day bereavement leave his company had given him when his father died after a long battle with cancer. He was understandably sad and a little distracted when his employer said: "Your bereavement leave is done. Now get over it and get back to work." People, especially those who have not experienced the death of a loved one, can have unrealistic expectations based on their lack of experience or empathy. In these cases, although hurtful, you must consider the source and know that your timeline is not contingent on anyone else.

After Jacques, my first husband, died, it took about nine months before I could truly connect with anyone else. I did go back to work, but I didn't want to be close or share too much with others. After Ron, my second husband, died, my recovery was somewhat quicker. My son moved in with me after four months, and not being alone made a huge difference.

People say it will take a month, a year, or even five years to get over the passing of a loved one. Other people say that grief takes as long as it takes, and to those newly grieving or those experiencing their first transition of a loved one, such uncertain advice can be horrifying, leaving them thinking that the immense pain they are feeling right now may never end. I encourage people by saying that each day they will feel a little better than the day before, and at their own speed, they will evolve into someone who no longer misses but fondly remembers their loved one. I say you never get over it, but you do learn to go forward with your life, and you always keep a place in your heart for your loved one that remains precious eternally.

MOVING THROUGH GRIEVING PRACTICE

How long it takes you to move through grieving can be influenced by many factors such as:

1. If the death of a loved one is the first you have experienced.
2. If the death was sudden.
3. If the death was by suicide.

4. If the death was caused by violence.
5. If you have known others who have died from the same cause.
6. If the death was a child.
7. If the death was the result of an illness.
8. If the death was long and drawn out.
9. If the death was preventable.
10. If you were there when it happened.

Any one of these situations can influence how long or how difficult your grief may remain. Each one has its own unique circumstances that affect us differently and add stress, concern, and even guilt to the grieving process.

Other factors affecting how long you actively grieve are:

1. Your religious beliefs.
2. Previous losses you have experienced.
3. Difficulty accepting loss.
4. How you are related to the one who died.
5. Cultural beliefs.
6. Dealing with issues like depression.
7. Your support system.
8. How well you take care of yourself and your health.
9. How you feel about the afterlife
10. How you process emotions.

When you experience a combination of these factors, your grieving process may become more challenging. Added conditions can slow the process down or intensify it greatly. Either way, being aware of all the conditions around your loss can help you see the many layers and complexities it entails. Therefore, overcoming it takes time and self-care.

Take some time right now to consider how your grief has been progressing. You may want to use your journal to track your timeline so you can see how far you are progressing. You may want to ask yourself:

* *How do any of the items on these lists relate to your loss specifically?*
* *Do you feel stuck in any of your experiences?*
* *Do you feel like there are things you need to deal with before you move forward?*

   *   *Do any of the items on the list relate to your grief? If so, is there something you can do about that?*

The Journal of the American Medical Association (JAMA)[3] in 2007 said: "Yale researchers found that on average the symptoms of grief peaked in six months and diminished during the year." These numbers are based on averages of the people surveyed, and they are only a frame of reference to consider. With my mother's death, two years passed before I started feeling more like I had before her illness. When Jacques died after I had been caring for him for two years, it took more than a year before I felt like I could start getting involved with the world again. When Ron died, I did better since I had those experiences in the past, and I knew Ron was ready for his transition. That knowing in me made a big difference once he was gone.

I still grieved deeply when my second husband died, and when the first year of grieving subsided, I decided to go on a big international trip. The trip was a tour with people who shared a common interest in ceramics, and it was a wonderful experience. I had dreamed for years about traveling through Tuscany, and two weeks of visiting the international ceramics show and watching ceramic artists create in their studios was a dream come true. I also got to create ceramics of my own in the most beautiful outdoor setting. I made new friends and came home inspired to start creating in my studio again, a joy I hadn't been able to participate in during Ron's last two years of life. When I returned home, my friends all commented that I looked happier and healthier than they had seen in a long time.

You will experience different levels of feelings that will ebb and flow. You might wonder why you are crying at some point, and other times wonder how you could possibly be smiling. The key is to observe yourself without judgment. Writing regularly in your journal can help you reflect on how those ups and downs affect you. Or how they begin to be further apart and less intense.

Some people grieve deeply for more than a year. While prolonged deep mourning is unusual, it can happen. Many of us become sad during holidays or cry when our favorite love song comes on the radio. That's not prolonged

---

[3] https://medicine.yale.edu/news-article/yearning-most-salient-feeling-following-a-loss/

grieving. That is remembering with love. My mother had prolonged grieving after my father died. They had been married 52 years, and she didn't know how to function without him. When she didn't get better and seemed to keep getting sadder, we took her to the doctor, who ran tests. We discovered that she had a brain tumor which was causing some of her symptoms. I am not suggesting that the tumor was the cause for prolonged grieving, but when your feelings seem to be getting worse after a year and include other symptoms, seeing a medical doctor is a good idea.

Always consider the circumstances. If you are a single mother of an only child and that child dies, your loss is different than if you have been caring for an elderly parent who has been sick for years, and again, different still from a spouse whose partner was killed by a drunk driver. The key is not to judge or compare. You are on your path, as everyone else is on theirs. If you think someone else is grieving for too long, do something kind for them; demonstrate love. If you feel you are grieving for too long, do something kind for yourself to move you forward.

In Maui, a honeymooner went to scout a hike he wanted to take his new wife on, but he fell off a cliff and died. A friend of mine, her husband was killed tragically in a plane crash. Another friend was ill and in hospice for almost 40 days. While writing this book, the young graphic designer who was helping me complete it was killed in a fire. We never know when our time here will be up. Embracing every moment will help us keep our lives in perspective and appreciate our journey. Instead of considering how long your grieving timeline will take, consider what you must do today to help you deal with your situation. Only you know how much time you need to process your loss.

Grief is a normal reaction to loss. Many things can affect how long you actively grieve about something. The key is to not judge yourself for how long it takes you to grieve or to judge yourself for what you are grieving. And don't judge anyone else in their grieving. You may grieve more intently if your car is destroyed in an accident even though no one was hurt. You may grieve if your scrapbooks with all the memories of your children are destroyed when your water heater bursts. You may grieve if a friend stops calling or goes on with their life, forgetting your pain. Grief is affected by many factors that can become overwhelming at the time of someone's death. I did not realize that my mother had forgotten how to pay bills or do banking long before I discovered her health was compromised. I was overwhelmed when I stepped in to fix things and realized her financial situation was a mess.

You can grieve for a person who has Alzheimer's or is in a coma even though they haven't died yet, and you may feel guilty for feeling that way. Sometimes we can't tell whether a person can really hear us, understand us, or know that we are there, so treating them like they can hear and understand is the most compassionate thing you can do for them and yourself.

You may have difficulty dealing with the situation when your last words with your loved one were angry or false. You can't know when what you say is the last thing someone hears. If you aren't happy with the last thing you said, forgive yourself. Forgiveness is important.

The length of grieving can be affected if the one grieving has been affected by the abuse of the person who died. The damage done by the abuse can continue and even worsen if it is not dealt with. Abuse happens more often than we would care to think about it. The abuse does not have to be physical; other forms of abuse can prolong and intensify grief.

When death comes after a long illness, you may have been having anticipatory grief and feel relieved when the person actually transitions. The key here is to recognize that it's okay if you are relieved that someone you loved dies under these circumstances. Feeling relieved doesn't negate your grief. You can be glad that the suffering is over while you miss being with them. Your feelings can be unpredictable while grieving. Don't judge yourself for anything you are experiencing. No magic amount of time will pass, and then suddenly, you realize you are no longer grieving. Chances are that you won't stop grieving no matter how much time has passed. The good news is that love remains even after their body transitions.

My heart is full because I will always carry the love of my husbands, my parents, the rest of my family, and all my friends who have died. I grieved them being gone, but I also love the time they were in my life. With each loss, the intensity of grief tended to lessen faster. It happened gradually until one day I realized I was breathing easier, smiling more, and focusing on what I was feeling at that moment.

You will get to that point, also. Allow yourself that time. As your grief lessens, you will remember the sweet memories and love you have experienced with your loved one, and begin to see the joy and beauty in each day.

Practice: Journaling Your Timeline

Journaling can help you to express your thoughts so that you can deal with them. Try exploring your timeline with loss in your journal. *When did you have peaks and valleys? How long did they last? Are they becoming further apart? How does your timeline compare with anyone else you know? Do you feel that you are where you should be in your grieving timeline?* If you are, that's wonderful. If you are not, *what can you do to make things better?* Take some time to explore how you are feeling and if there is anything you can do to improve your situation.

Key Tips for Chapter Two

* Everyone progresses through their grieving transformation at their own pace.
* Take time to deal with your loss in your own way.
* Know there will come a time when your loss becomes filled with loving memories instead of an overwhelming obstacle.

TAKE ACTION

HAPPINESS HABITS

Your Intention

* Write an *Intention* about moving forward from now in your grief timeline.

I intend to _____

_____

_____

_____

_____

Your Gratitude

* Write what you are *grateful* for concerning your grief timeline.

I am happy and grateful that _____

_____

_____

_____

_____

Your Happiness

* In relation to what you read about your grief timeline, what are you anticipating will bring your *happiness* as you move forward in dealing with your grief?

_____

_____

_____

_____

_____

Your Affirmation

* Write a positive *affirmation* about what you are changing in your life relating to your grief timeline.

I am _____

_____

_____

_____

_____

_____

CHAPTER 3

LOVE

"Make the impossible possible by loving."
-STEVIE WONDER

Love is part of grief. There would be no grief if there were no love. Love exists amongst grief, and grief comes from loving the other person. Even though the path of your relationship may not have always been easy with them, the time you spent together is filled with important memories. Cherish the good memories you shared.

When you think of love, what are you thinking? Does your love have conditions? We say we love different people or situations, but *what does that really mean to you?* Here are some different kinds of love to think of:

1. The love of a parent
2. The love of a child
3. The love of a relative
4. The love of a friend
5. The love of or for a pet
6. The love of whatever higher power you believe in

How many of these different kinds of loves have you experienced or are you experiencing? How many of them are conditional? As a child, I felt the love of my parents was conditional. If only I could do better in school, they would love me more. I always craved love and attention that was never demonstrated, and I missed out on feeling unconditional love until I had my own children. I have had pets I have loved unconditionally who brought me love and joy. And I have had pets that I wanted to feel more love for; if only they would stop digging holes in my yard and tearing up my garden hoses. I had a friend that I really wanted to love if only he could be truthful with me. *How many loves have you had that have the feelings "if only" attached to them?*

UNCONDITIONAL VERSUS CONDITIONAL LOVE

Consider what love really means to you. Ron and I used to have talks about love because much of the love I experienced had been conditional. We agreed that being honest with each other was essential and that there was no room for being judgmental in our relationship. As a result of our communication, I chose to commit to loving him and all things unconditionally. I didn't realize unconditional love would be challenging, but I have come a long way. I could easily say I loved unconditionally, but then I'd catch myself judging someone, and that's not unconditional love.

I remembered the words of Elisabeth Kubler Ross: "When you don't choose love, you choose fear." Many philosophers say that love and fear are the only two real emotions, and I knew I didn't want to live in fear. When it came to love, I realized that at times I was afraid someone wouldn't love me, or love me enough, if I didn't behave a certain way, if I didn't do something they thought I was supposed to, or if I didn't look my best by putting on make-up or wearing certain clothes. When I realized what I was doing to gain love, I was surprised at myself. I started writing a list of what I love about myself, and soon I knew *I am enough the way I am.* Learning that I love myself allowed me to enjoy and progress in my life. It freed me to soar forward and discover true happiness.

In the words of John Lennon,

> *"There are two basic motivating forces: fear and love. When*
> *we are afraid, we pull back from life. When we are in love,*
> *we open to all life offers with passion, excitement, and acceptance.*

We must learn to love ourselves first, in all our glory and imperfections.
If we cannot love ourselves, we cannot fully open to our ability
to love others or our potential to create. Evolution and all hopes
for a better world rest is the fearlessness and open-hearted vision
of people who embrace life."

Love starts with you! Think about all the things in life you have been afraid of, such as not having enough money in your paycheck to cover your bills, falling for someone you aren't sure of trusting, or being afraid to go out to dinner by yourself because you're worried of what people will think. *How much have you missed out on life because of your fear?*

Now is the time to let go of those fears. Try making a commitment to love your life unconditionally, with all its flaws. Right now, at this moment, you are alive, you are hopefully healthy, and if you sat in gratitude, you would realize that you have more blessings than you can count. Life is good right now! *If you are feeling grief in your life, what can you do to help your situation?* When you live in the mindset of love, you will find yourself smiling more and seeing things to be happy for.

You may say that is all good in theory, but I still miss my child, parent, or partner, and that is to be expected. Missing someone can create opportunities to bring more love into your life. When a drunk driver killed Leigh's son as he was riding his bike to the store on an errand for her, she turned her devastation into great work by creating *Mothers Against Drunk Drivers*™. She chose to serve other mothers experiencing a similar circumstance as her. When my mother died, I became a conservator for her sister who I developed a deep, loving relationship with, being responsible for all her needs until she died. Love helped me care for her till the end.

I wasn't sure I could ever fall in love again when Jacques died. So, when I met Ron after Jacques had been gone a year and a half, I thought I was ready to begin a new relationship but my heart kept telling me I was still married. I had not gotten a divorce, and though our wedding vows said, "Until death do you part," I didn't feel un-married after Jacques died. I deeply loved Ron, but it took me four years before I could actually get married to him. I knew there was no preset timeline and that I wanted to love and be loved again. Then, one day, I realized that I had relaxed into the comfort of truly loving myself as l am, and I realized that I do extend unconditional love to everyone knowing that it is not my business to judge or fear them. An old Hawaiian saying is, "Love takes time. Loss takes longer."

Many of us go through life as our own worst critics. We think we weigh too much or too little; we don't smile enough or laugh too much. Our wardrobe doesn't flatter us the way we would like it to. We are too tall or too short. Our hair is too curly or too straight. We are too shy or too outgoing. We allow that voice in our hearts to run rampant, convincing us we are not worthy of the self-love we seek. Self-condemnation puts up a giant roadblock to living life in love. The good news is that recognizing your actions is a giant step forward in improving your situation.

Presently, Ron has been gone for some time. I still miss him and find comfort in writing letters to him. When I write these letters, I am reminded of the long conversations we had and what advice he would be giving me. Friends who live close to me are wonderful musicians, and I love to attend their gigs. On Sunday evenings, they play at a club where I sit outside and witness amazing sunsets over the ocean and the west Maui mountains. The last time I went to one of their events, someone I didn't know came up and asked me to dance. I hesitated because dancing was something I loved to do with Ron. I surprised myself, though, as I said yes without a moment's thought. While I enjoyed dancing, I found that I couldn't look at the man I was dancing with. When the song was over, he came, sat with me, and bought me a drink, club soda with lots of lime, my favorite designated-driver drink! We started talking, and I found myself disturbingly judging things he said. *Why was I judging?* This behavior is *so* not me! I realized that it was because he was not my Ron. I took a deep breath, forgave myself, and went on to have a nice conversation.

As you go through the period of what seems like a constant transition, be mindful of what you say, what you do, and what you wish for. Be open to new experiences and be easy on yourself when you meet new people. You may find yourself judging people based on what you perceive about them. If your situation is like Leigh's, whose son was killed by a drunk driver, don't recoil because you see someone with a glass of wine. If you see a friend enjoying the company of her mother, recognize if you jump to jealousy because you can't hold your mother's hand and share your secrets with her. Be happy for your friend so that she can spend time with her mother, and forgive yourself for your temporary lapse. The more love you genuinely broadcast, the more love will flow back to you abundantly. Live your life in love *always*. Being willing to love and start now.

PRACTICE: UNCONDITIONAL LOVE

Write a love letter where you fully express your unconditional love. First, choose who you will write the letter to. You may write it to your loved one who died, to yourself, to your child, or to a friend who you haven't spoken to in years. Whoever you choose, before you write, think about why you chose the person and what it is that you want to express. Take your time with the letter to find the right words for you to share. You may want to meditate and/ or pray before you start writing.

Be in absolute truth as you write, clearly expressing yourself so that your words leave no doubt to the recipient. After writing your letter, put it aside for a day or so, then read it aloud. When you are comfortable saying everything you want to, mail your letter. If you wrote it to yourself or your loved one who died, put it in a special place to save and read again whenever you could use loving support.

After you write the letter, write some notes on how you feel about writing the letter. *What did you learn? How can you incorporate more love into your life?*

KEY TIPS FOR CHAPTER THREE

* Love does not end with death.
* Love that was shared can still be cherished.
* Grief is a part of love.

TAKE ACTION

HAPPINESS HABITS

Your Intention

* Write an *Intention* about experiencing more love in your life.

I intend to _____

_____

_____

_____

_____

Your Gratitude

* Write what you are *grateful* for about three people you love.

I am happy and grateful that _____

_____

_____

_____

_____

Your Happiness

* In relation to what you read about love, what loving relationship are you experiencing now, who is it with, and why does it make you happy?

_____

_____

_____

_____

_____

Your Affirmation

* Write a positive *affirmation* about the unconditional love you are experiencing.

I am _____

_____

_____

_____

_____

_____

PERSONAL NOTES

CHAPTER 4

GIVE YOURSELF PERMISSION TO DO WHAT YOU WANT

"Don't be afraid to be phenomenal. Claim your greatness."
−REV. CAROLYN WILLIAMS

During the grieving process, we often feel like we *should* be doing the *right* thing. I want you to give yourself permission right now to do what you have always wanted to do. Give yourself full reign to experience whatever that is. *Do you want to cut your hair? Do you want to go on a cruise? Do you want to have a party? Do you want to have a marvelous spa day? Do you want to take a ceramics class? Do you want to travel to visit your friend? Do you want to go fishing all day or ride the coastline in a fancy convertible car?* It doesn't matter what it is; I encourage you to move in that direction so that you can experience the joy that it will bring you. Move through the hesitation and just do it!

Try starting small. Get a little notebook or open a file on your computer. Then brainstorm a list of all the things you would like to do. Don't judge anything as you write it down; add new things that feel enjoyable to your list. Include things you have already done but would like to do more of. Maybe you took a cake decorating class years ago and loved it but haven't made it in a long time. Add *decorate a cake* to your list, and don't worry about who it will be for, how you will decorate it, or what flavor it will be. Instead, write down "decorate a cake."

Maybe you started reading a series of books in the past, and you didn't finish reading the whole series, something like the *Maisie Dobbs Mystery* series or *The Number One Ladies' Detective Agency* series (both of which I highly recommend!) Put the series' name on your list, and you'll know whether you want to start or finish the series.

Write down everything you can think of, no matter how big or how small. Include the places you've always wanted to travel, the classes you've always wanted to take, the recipes you've always wanted to make, and the friends you always meant to stay in touch with. The things you've wanted to build and the new experiences you've longed to enjoy. Keep writing until you think you are out of ideas, then write some more. Sometimes the best ideas come after you have cleared out all the things that surface quickly.

Once you have your list, set it aside for a day or two. When you return to it, see if you have thought of other things to add. Use a highlighter to identify the things you'd like to do immediately—then start doing them! It's as easy as that. I've put my whole list in order, with the things I want to do the most at the top. And from the list, I create another separate list of long-term desires, such as a big trip, that I won't necessarily do right away but I will start planning for.

I created a long list and prioritized it, making it easier for me to do things on the list instead of trying to figure out what to do next. I did big things like plan and go on two trips I had always dreamed of, one to Tuscany and one to Bali. I pursued other things, such as participating in a quilting class, going to lectures at the University, having dinner with friends, and taking lots of books to the *Friends of the Library* events. Eventually, I didn't rely on my list as I discovered that it had encouraged me to subconsciously immerse myself in *taking care of myself* and enjoying the momentum!

When I asked friends of mine who were grieving what they've always wanted to do, my friend Carla said, "I have always wanted to experience the magical lights of the Aurora Borealis. The natural world at its most astonishing!" My trainer Ellis has always wanted to go on a vacation for a week by himself without television. He told me he had never been on a vacation. Both of those things sounded like good things to do, and I encouraged them each to do them. Think about what you'd want to do more than anything else, and plan for it now!

As you create your list, consider what *you* love to do, not what someone else suggests you do. Think about the things that make you happy. I found that doing creative things comforted me the best. I loved the feeling of the clay in my hands as I did ceramic sculpture and watched the figures as they emerged. I learned to draw, something that I always thought I couldn't do. I got lost in spending time in nature, drawing tropical plants and flowers, and always felt refreshed when I finished. Doing new things helped me see life through a new lens. It stimulated my mind in a fresh new way and formed new memories, experiences, and feelings that made me feel again.

ACTIVITIES TO UPLIFT YOUR SPIRIT

Here is a fabulous list of lots of different things to think of that you might want to do. When you think of other things, let me know. I would love to see what you are up to!

* **Find a series on television that interests you and binge-watch it.** Get a bowl of popcorn or a crochet project to work on, and get lost in it and enjoy. I highly recommend *The Crown*™, *Genius American*™ drama series, or *Call the Midwife*™. Regular television series are good too, like *Gray's Anatomy*™, *Ted Lasso*™, *Only Murders in the Building*™, or *Beat Bobby Flay*™. Pick something that interests you and immerse yourself in it.

* **Get all your pictures together and make a scrapbook.** You can get fancy with all kinds of materials from the craft store or create a collection of your pictures on your computer. Or you can pick pictures you love and write stories or memories about the pictures or the times they were taken. And you can make it in a way you could duplicate it for gifts, maybe one for your best friend and one for you, or a copy for each of your close family members for Christmas presents.

* **Try a new food.** Either ask a friend or go out to lunch, or try a recipe at home with the goal of eating something you haven't tried before.

So many of us eat the same thing day after day. Try something new to introduce you to flavors you haven't tasted before. I went to a vegan restaurant and tried a raw "bagel" with cashew jalapeño cream cheese. It was so good; I had to return a few times to have it again! Try a new ethnic food. Maybe you haven't had Ethiopian food or food from a Kosher deli. Google restaurants or recipes and see what strikes your fancy. Or find a bakery that has Kouign-Amann. It is amazing!

* **Take or give a cooking class.** When I was in Madrid, I took a class on how to make the famous Tapas of Spain. The teacher even modified it for me to be vegetarian. The Spanish tortilla and Sangria were especially good! In New Orleans, I learned to cook red beans, rice, and bread pudding with bourbon sauce. After that, I took a Vegan Chef certification program, and I invited my friends to my house to try preparing vegan recipes. Their favorite dishes were tuna-less salad and chocolate "cream" tofu pie. (Email me and I'll share my recipes!)

* **Find a buddy.** I met Sarah at a Death Cafe. We went to a fun workshop together, hung out at the beach, and talked for hours. Being with someone who has also had a loss can be very freeing, You can be completely comfortable with each other because of your common understanding. We were able to talk about things others wouldn't comprehend. A buddy can help.

* **Host a Dinner Party where you live.** Dinner parties are popping up all over the country where groups of 20- to 30-year-olds who have experienced a loss get together for a potluck on a regular basis. You can find them online. If that isn't your age group, start your own. You can find people in a group you attend by posting your idea on Facebook™ or creating a Meet-Up™ group. Or you can only invite people you know who are also mourning. Have a theme like Soup and Salad or Italian food, and have a sign-up so you don't get all the same dishes! Make it fun and relaxing.

* **Read and meditate.** My husband and I always read and meditated in the morning. Friends started joining us, and now that he is gone, our little group lives on. People have come and gone, and one friend

joins us by phone every morning. I love starting my day with such peace!

* **Learn a new sport that gets you outdoors.** My husband loved to golf, and when my friends asked me to join them in a beginner's class, he was so happy that he bought me a set of clubs! Unfortunately, that was right before his health took a turn, but I think now is the time for me to learn. Anything that gets you outdoors is good. I love to walk with friends or by myself. Whether it is at the park, on a forest trail, at the beach, or in the neighborhood, walking is refreshing, build strength and lung capacity by breathing in all that fresh air!

* **Get online.** I enjoy taking pictures when I go on my walks around Maui. There is so much beauty here. I post them regularly on Instagram and love making new friends there. I also like to read about what's happening with everyone I know on social media. I have reconnected there with people I have known throughout my life, and I love seeing what has happened with them. I also write a blog about my experiences. Writing is healing for me, and I hope what I post is helping others. I'd love for you to sign up on my website for my blog.

* **Create your own rituals.** I like to drink a cup of tea each day. I try different kinds for variety. You could light candles when you do meditation or when you take a relaxing bath. You could light a fire and have a cup of hot chocolate while you read or write in your journal. A friend told me about John, who washes his wife's car every week even though she isn't there to drive anymore. Find something comforting you can do on a regular basis that you can look forward to as your special time with yourself.

* **Clean your home.** Cleaning can actually be fun and interesting. I love sorting through things to get rid of or picking a cupboard, closet, drawer, or dresser to go through and make it more organized. I find things I didn't know I had and release things I realize I don't need. After I am done sorting, I know where to find things! Maybe the task of something like washing windows seems daunting, but if you do one or two windows a week, they'll all be clean in no time!

* **Volunteer.** *Do you love holding babies?* Call your local hospital and see if they need help. *Do you love cooking?* See if you can cook at the local women's shelter once a week. *Do you love to paint?* See if you can teach a class for local foster children. *Do you love to walk on the beach?* Take a garbage bag with you and clean as you go. *Do you love to read?* Call a local elementary school and see if you can read books out loud to the students. *Do you love to walk?* See if your local animal shelter has a way you can take the dogs for a walk with you. Think of all the things you love or would love to do, and I am sure there is a place in the community where you could provide some additional help.

* **Take care of others.** The ladies who live next door have mobility issues. I've been taking their newspaper up to their door every day, which doesn't seem like a big thing, but they appreciate not having to walk out to the driveway and bend over to get it. Maybe you have a neighbor that could use a break from her children. Bring them to your house to bake cookies or play games so the mom can have some downtime. If you know someone who can't drive, take them out to lunch or drive them to buy groceries or to an appointment. Organize a group of friends to provide food for someone who had surgery or who suffered a loss. You don't have to do something big. Think of what you would love for someone else to do for you if you were in their shoes.

* **Schedule things that bring you pleasure.** When the catalog of classes at the local arts center comes out, I go through it right away and sign up for something fun each time. I know I will go when it's on my calendar, and I've paid for it. Local community centers have activities you may want to try. I always notice the ballroom dancers at the local cultural center. Someday I'll sign up for a dance class. If you have always wanted to draw, paint, surf, hike, dance, or anything else, sign up and go! And also schedule things like massages, facials, pedicures, or lunch or tea with a friend. Go to a car rally, a museum, or an antiques show. *What brings you pleasure?*

* **Take a class online.** You can learn something entirely different from anything you have studied before. Many universities offer free

classes online to people of all ages. I took a free class from Stanford University on Creativity. Students from all over the world came up with such imaginative projects. Stanford offers over 160 free classes like Language, Living on the Nuclear Brink, and Introduction to Computer Networking. Google™ for classes on any subject you'd like to learn more about and see what comes up.

* **Do the things you once enjoyed.** I met Nina, a ceramic artist, on my trip to Tuscany, and she said that clay was her refuge. She got lost in the feeling of creating something beautiful. When I am on the potter's wheel or hand-building something in clay, I get totally lost and have no concept of time. Think of things to do that you haven't done in a while. Build a model, crochet a blanket, audition for a play, take a tap dancing class, work on a political campaign, join a gardening club, create a community garden, become a docent at a local gallery or planetarium, join a singles group at your church and make some new supportive friends. You can do anything you want to.

The key to making this list is to find things to do that nourish your soul, that are positive, and bring you joy. Take care of your social self as well as your private self. Over time, you can discover the growth that comes from your experiences and the new you you are becoming. Take a deep breath, and step forward into something new.

PRACTICE: PLAY DATE

Doing activities with friends can enhance your experience. I met a new friend whose husband died shortly after mine. We decided to keep each other company when we wanted to explore new things. We've gone to concerts, done art classes, and hosted parties. I found I am more likely to do things when I don't have to go alone.

When my children were little, I used to arrange times when they could get together with friends to do something fun. Well, you're never too old for a play date! So, choose a friend and find an activity you both enjoy and do it!

You can start by listing friends or people you would like to get to know better. Then make a list of things you would have fun doing. Then compare the lists to see who would be best for each experience. You want to choose people that will add to your adventure and have the same interests. Maybe one friend would be perfect to take a class with, while another friend would be perfect to plant a vegetable garden with. Or, maybe you could get a small group of friends together and brainstorm some ideas to have fun together.

The sky's the limit here. You may start something regular, like a weekly walking group or a monthly book club. Soon you'll be doing the things you've always wanted to enjoy and doing it with people you love and care about.

Key Tips for Chapter Four

* Trying new things is a healthy way to move forward.
* Explore new things to try.
* Do something special for you.

Take Action

HAPPINESS HABITS

Your Intention

* Write an *Intention* about something new you will do or learn about.

I intend to _____

_____

_____

_____

_____

_____

Your Gratitude

* Write what you are *grateful* for about three new people you have met or three new things you are learning to do.

I am happy and grateful that _____

_____

_____

_____

_____

_____

Your Happiness

* In relation to what you read in this chapter about giving yourself permission, what will you now give yourself permission for, and why do you know this will bring you *happiness*?

_____

_____

_____

_____

_____

Your Affirmation

* Write a positive *affirmation* about what you are giving yourself permission to do.

I am _____

_____

_____

_____

_____

_____

_____

CHAPTER 5

THE POWER OF JOURNALING

*"I can shake off everything as I write: my sorrows disappear,
my courage is reborn."*
—ANNE FRANK

Grief can be an isolating experience, but it doesn't have to be. Your journal can be your constant companion to share thoughts with and explore more intimately what you are feeling. Your journal can also improve your mood when you focus on writing about things that make you happy. I made a regular practice of journaling after my husband died to help support my fluctuating emotions. Now I journal every day and look forward to the comfort it brings. My journal is my best friend, always there for me, willing to listen to anything I need to say. I can confide in my journal how I used to have long conversations with my husbands.

Power journaling is pouring your heart onto the page as you become aware of what matters in your life, of what your heart desires. Power journaling involves continuous and vigorous sharing on the page without any filtering or holding back. Some people power journal each day and tap into deeper self-knowing as they express their feelings openly and without any apprehensions. Power journaling gives you permission to write anything and everything free of judgments and grammatical corrections. It is often called freewriting as you tap into your more subconscious thinking. Committing to this style of writing in your journal is committing to self-care, which can be essential in leading you forward through your grief.

Journaling allows us to give a break to what Buddhists call the 'Monkey mind,' or what Eckhart Tolle calls the 'voice in the head where your ego calls the shots.' Our egos are so focused on themselves that they tell us that we can't do anything right because they are in charge. Picture the ego as a little person puffed up with how great it is bouncing around in your empty skull, constantly distracting you with stress, anxiety, and negativity. Journaling can bring you that peace as it draws your focus into what you *want* to think about or explore. Daily journaling permits you to shut out ineffective thoughts and emotions that do not serve you and welcome powerful new thoughts that will ideally bring you peace.

WHY KEEP A JOURNAL?

Here is a list of many of the benefits of journal writing. Journaling allows you to:

* Get to know yourself more deeply.
* Discover your purpose.
* Clear your thoughts no matter what they are.
* Cultivate mindfulness.
* Discover happiness.
* Explore who you really are.
* Celebrate you and your experiences and milestones.
* Quiet your mind.
* Become grounded.
* Reduce your stress.
* Process emotions.
* Find clarity.
* Help cope with your loss.
* Overcome fears.
* Cope with your grief experience.

* Bring order to chaos in your life.
* Improve your health.
* Help regulate your physical health.
* Make choices.
* Keep track of your dreams.
* Foster personal growth.

Establishing a Journaling Practice

After my husband died, I started writing daily in my journal. I wrote about how I was feeling, and what I wanted to discover about what I would do now that I was alone. The more I wrote, the better I felt. I started doing things that I uncovered in my writing, like inviting people to come to my home and write about grief with me, which proved to be comforting for all who participated.

You may have tried to start a journaling practice or writing in a diary; about half the people out there have 'tried' to do it. If that is the case, I encourage you not to *try* this time but to, in fact, follow through and succeed at it. Begin by considering what you want to accomplish by journaling. *Are you exploring your thoughts or feelings? Are you writing memories you are concerned you may forget? Are you trying to work out the issues you have?* Start writing what will serve you emotionally and see where that sharing leads you.

When you are ready to clear your thoughts, increase your focus, and uplift your energy, it's time to start a journaling practice. Commit to a practice that will suit you as an effective means of self-care. As you get started, here are some things to consider:

* **Carefully choose the journal you want to write in**. You may want a beautiful, handmade leather book or one with a meaningful saying or image on the front. Or you may find an inexpensive blank book that appeals to you. I use a composition notebook with a black and white cover that I get a good bargain on at back-to-school sales every year. That's how much I write.

* **Choose a special pen that is comfortable for you.** I have tried different colors, yet I always return to a beautiful blue. You can also choose from several pens and pick the one that suits your mood for what you are writing that day. Love the feel of the pen and the way the ink flows.

* **You may want to write on your electronic device, setting up a file to use only for journaling.** I sometimes journal on the *Notes App* on my phone while away from my journal or computer, and creativity strikes. There are many journaling apps to choose from in the app store on your phone. Notebook™, Word™, and Google can also be used. Use what works for you.

* **Experiment with recording an audio or video journal dictating your thoughts.** Choose the method of writing or recording that suits you best. You can use your phone, a microphone attached to your computer, a dictator, or a good, old-fashioned handheld recording device. Remember, journaling is for you, not anyone else.

* **Journaling doesn't require perfection.** Be messy when you want to. Cross out words you changed your mind about. Spelling doesn't matter if you can tell what the word is supposed to be. No one will grade your journal, and likely no one will ever see what your write there. Your handwriting doesn't need to be perfect either.

* **Don't edit. Editing while you write breaks up your thoughts.** Be free of needing to edit as if you are writing a paper. And don't rush your writing, there are no time limits to journaling. No one is looking over your shoulder. Journaling isn't meant to be graded; it is meant to be enjoyed.

* **There is no pressure in journaling.** Write as much as you want to, whenever you want, for as long as you want. You set the tone, the pace, and the duration. Allow it to be fun, relaxing, and personal.

* **Fit journaling into your regular routine.** Writing in your journal every day will serve you the best. Many people do it first thing in the morning when their thoughts are not influenced by the day. Others

journal in the evening and write about the events that unfolded. Anytime is the right time; pick a time that will allow you to be consistent.

* **Choose the time of day you want to journal regularly.** Choose a time that will provide the most peace and quiet. I love to journal first thing in the morning, where I ask myself what my intention is for the day, recall something that brought me joy the day before, and always list things I am grateful for. Other people like to journal right before bed to clear their thoughts before they sleep.

* **Choose a place to journal that suits you best.** I sit up in bed to journal in the morning. You may have a special chair to relax in or a seat on your porch that you love and enjoy. You may want to take your journal with you on your daily walk and sit under a tree or on a favorite bench as you journal. You may want to write sitting in different places, like in front of your altar or sitting on a hill looking out at the vista. Be sure the place you choose is peaceful and quiet.

* **Put your phone on airplane mode so you won't be disturbed.** Pings and notifications from your phone can be a distraction, as can outside calls and interruptions. Give yourself the gift of journalling uninterrupted.

* **Make a commitment to yourself.** Think about what you want to do to make your practice of journal writing sustainable. Decide that you are important and make this process a valuable part of your healing. You deserve to feel wonderful.

* **Be willing to practice.** If you think you can't figure out what to write, set a timer starting with a short amount of time, as short as five minutes, and commit to writing. Then set the timer for a little more time every day until you reach the time that works best for you, for example, fifteen minutes to half an hour. Journaling is a process that may take a bit of practice in the beginning. Whenever we start something new, we need to give ourselves time to get good at it.

READY TO WRITE

"Fill your paper with the breathings of your heart."
WILLIAM WORDSWORTH

Creating a journaling practice that works for you is a positive, supportive act of self-care that is easy to do and cost-free. What you write in your journal is private, only for you. I can hear you saying, *But I don't know what to write!* My answer to that is, *Yes, you do.* You need to be open to your thoughts and allow yourself to express them.

Each time you are ready to start writing in your journal, take a moment to close your eyes, take a few deep breaths, and allow what you will be writing to come to you gently. Journaling is easy the more that you do it, and I am certain it will become a staple in your routine. Allow yourself to infuse authenticity into your writing.

The first thing you write in your new journal can be a commitment to create and follow a writing practice that works best for you. Your commitment can include making a promise to yourself to write every day, to only write to tell yourself the truth, and to be open in whatever you write, even when it surprises you.

When you are ready to write, try these steps to get started:

* **Write the purpose you want from writing in your journal.**
  * Try different ideas like exploring your thoughts or your heart, expressing all you are feeling, or finding comfort.
  * Decide which of your ideas best expresses your purpose.
* **When you decide what you want to use for your purpose, write it as a direct statement. For instance:**
  * I explore my thoughts (or my heart) in my journal.
  * I express what I am feeling in my journal.
  * I find comfort in writing in my journal.

* **Always use the first person when writing in your journal:**
  * I explore
  * I express
  * I find
* **When you can use positive words.**
  * For instance, instead of saying, "I am not sad," say, "I am happy," or "I feel happiness some of the time."
  * Write words that make you smile.

Remember that you are free to write anything you want in your journal without expectations. There is no right or wrong to journaling; you never have to share it with anyone unless you want to.

IDEAS FOR WHAT TO WRITE

I start my journal daily with a ritual. First, I thank Energy or God for guidance and protection. Of course, you can ask anything or anyone for guidance. Then I welcome all the Guides I love to have inspiration from for their guidance. My Guides are always changing and range from my husbands, to my favorite teachers, to my departed friends, depending on what I am writing about or exploring. I ask my Guides what I need to know that day.

Next, I write an *Intention* to focus on what I plan to accomplish. That is followed by at least three things that I am happy and grateful for. Sometimes there are much more than three things, and I rarely repeat my gratitude as I always find new things to appreciate in my life. I always include something that brought me joy the day before. Beginning my day by journaling daily gives me grounding in remembering how wonderful my life is. You could create a template to fill in what to write to get you started with the basic elements, including gratitude for your journaling process, what you want to discover, what miracles you have witnessed or been a part of, what you are grateful for, and what brings you joy.

After my basic journaling practice, I write anything I want to and follow the inspiration that guides my way. Journaling doesn't have to be the same every day. Here are some basic things you can write about to get you started:

PRACTICE WRITING

The more you write, the easier it becomes. Allow yourself to relax and escape into a peaceful place to thoroughly explore your thoughts. Write often using prompts like these to get you started.

Write your response to any of these questions:
* *What are you grateful for?*
* *What is your first memory?*
* *What has been your biggest challenge so far?*
* *What was the best day of your life?*
* *What makes you uncomfortable?*
* *What is your life's purpose?*
* *What three wishes do you have, and why do you have these wishes?*
* *What were you doing 5 years ago, and what will you be doing 5 years from now?*
* Write what is true about what you are experiencing.

LETTERS
Include who you are writing to and why:
* Write yourself a letter to when you were a younger age
* Write a motivational letter
* Write a letter of apology
* Write a love letter
* Write a letter to a loved one who died, then write a letter back to you from that person

LISTS
Items on your lists can give you endless things to write about:
* *What are your goals and how you will achieve them?*
* *What problems do you have and how will you solve them?*
* *What or who inspires you and why?*

* What negative thoughts do you have and how you can improve or solve them?
* Write everything you complained about today and why
* Write experiences you have had with synchronicity throughout your life
* What could you do better?
* What would you like to create?
* What books do you want to read and why?
* What are your most proud accomplishments?
* What do you dream about?

EXPERIENCES

What you experienced and the lessons learned:

* What brought you joy today and why?
* Mantras you have created for different experiences
* How you dealt with PTSD
* Explore your emotions
* What excited you and why?
* What are your favorite memories?
* What past wounds do you have and how can you heal them?
* Who do you need to forgive?
* Record instances of serendipity
* Write travel journals

A JOURNAL PRACTICE CHANGES YOUR LIFE

The benefits of our regular journal writing are never-ending. One you get into the groove of your practice, you will notice how your thoughts are clearer and you are more organized. Your 'monkey mind' will calm down and maybe even take a break! You will gain perspective on your life and know and understand yourself more. Your memory will improve, and your creativity will shine. I know from experience how much happiness you can cultivate for yourself in your journey of grief.

PRACTICE: JOURNALING, OF COURSE

Establish your new journaling practice by deciding what you want to write, how you will make that happen, and noticing what you are learning and experiencing in the process. Use all you learned in Chapter 5 to guide you.

KEY TIPS FOR CHAPTER FIVE

* Learn more about what happens with you as a result of your experiences.
* Celebrate your loved ones and your memories by writing about them.
* Journaling is an invaluable practice.

TAKE ACTION

HAPPINESS HABITS

Your Intention

* Write an *Intention* about how you are incorporating regular journaling into your life.

I intend to _____

_____

_____

_____

_____

_____

Your Gratitude

* Write what you are *grateful* for regarding what you anticipate you will learn in your journaling practice.

I am happy and grateful that _____

_____

_____

_____

_____

_____

Your Happiness

* In relation to what you read about journaling, *what are you anticipating will bring you happiness as you journal every day?*

_____

_____

_____

_____

Your Affirmation

* Write a positive *affirmation* about what you are changing in your life relating to writing about your grief.

I am _____

_____

_____

_____

_____

_____

CHAPTER 6

CRYING IN THE CAR

". . . you know that a good, long session of weeping can often make you feel better, even if your circumstances have not changed one bit."
—LEMONY SNICKET

Being alone in the car, for some reason, can trigger tears for me, and when it does, I cry, sob, or scream if I need to. I feel like sometimes I need to cleanse, to let the water run through me. If you cry in the car, you may or may not feel better after, but that does not matter. What does matter is that you do what you need to do, then move on.

When both of my husbands died, I had deep, uncontrollable sobs for a long time. What made such an intense experience easier was the love and support I received from my dear friends. However, most of my tears came when I was alone. My triggers varied widely, from seeing a butterfly to hearing a favorite song or having a sweet memory. Those tears seemed to be a release I had to endure, and I ultimately felt better afterward.

A few months after Jacques died, I found out our friend John had cancer and had gone to another city where he could get the treatment his diagnosis required. He died alone in his hotel room, waiting for treatment. At first, I was numb. I went to a gathering in his honor and had to leave early because my emotions were so strong. I sobbed for hours. I finally had a drink and another drink until I fell asleep. When I woke, I realized that alcohol was not a solution to my problem. I had never done anything like that before and felt terrible.

I vowed never to drink like that ever again. Yet, the deep sadness remained. I seemed to be grieving my friend and my husband at the same time. Life felt so fragile. That's when I realized it was time to get out of my head and find a way to move forward. I felt my emotions thoroughly and allowed myself all the crying they required.

Some people hold back their tears and block the outpouring of emotions that happens during grieving. Not crying may be harder on you than being able to release your tears. I think of it as if you have an open wound and put a heavy bandage over it. You don't want to see what it looks like under there, so you leave it until, ultimately, the wound festers and becomes enmeshed in the bandage. Removing the dressing creates much more pain, lasting longer than the initial wound. Tending to your emotions will allow them to heal versus allowing them to fester.

Only humans shed tears connected to emotions, which provides the vital function of releasing and regulating the body. When one has high blood pressure and a rapid pulse due to stress, both conditions can be lowered with tears. Tears can act as a physical reset or as releasing a pressure valve. Maybe you must shed some if you find that tears don't come easily. Try watching a sad movie or listening to a sad song and see what happens. Sometimes realizing you haven't cried will bring forth some tears. Everyone grieves differently, and not crying is not a cause to worry. When you are ready, your tears will come.

For some people, tears come easily, even too easily, interfering with trying to lead a normal life. If you know when you may cry, support yourself by being prepared.

* Excuse yourself to go to the restroom or an unoccupied room where you can be alone.
* Take a shower where no one will see or hear you crying.
* Go outside in nature, and be surrounded by Mother Earth and all of her support.
* Take a drive. Allow the tears to flow, and if needed pull off the road to let them pour.

If the tears come without warning, there are things that you can do to help:
* **Breathe.** The act of taking a slow deep breath can help you calm down and slow the tears.

* **Tissues.** Always keep tissues handy. When the tears and runny nose pour forth, you'll really want to catch them.
* **Wash your face.** Cool water can help let you breathe and relax. And it gives you something active to do.
* **Hugs.** If you are with someone you'd like comfort from, ask for a hug, or give them one. People usually would love to help and don't know what to do. They may cry also, and that's okay.
* **Tell it like it is.** If you are with people you don't know, tell the truth. They will understand; if they don't, it's their problem.

When tears come in public, take a moment to regroup. Take a short walk, stretch, and drink coffee or a glass of water. Then when your emotions have rebalanced, continue with what you were doing. Acknowledge and comfort your pain via some self-care—comfort food for dinner, taking a bath, swimming, walking, or doing something that feels indulgent and relaxing. Curl up with a good book or movie. Pamper yourself and know that the next day will be a new day.

Wherever the tears find you, know they are perfectly normal and a good release. I went to see the movie *Bohemian Rhapsody*™, and when it became obvious that in the true story, the lead singer, Freddie Mercury, was dying of AIDS, memories rushed back of several of my friends who died at that time, and I cried through most of the movie. Amazingly, after the movie, I felt kind of *reset*. I reminisced on all the positive memories I experienced with my friends, which felt good.

HISTORY INFLUENCES OUR TEARS

Your upbringing must also be considered in your grieving. When I was growing up, lots of family members died, and I don't recall seeing any tears. I thought I wasn't supposed to cry. I ended up crying into my pillow at night, thinking something was wrong with me. The key here is to be in tune with yourself. Even if your culture dictates grieving one way or another, do what you must, whether alone or with others.

Some of my friends shared their experiences with me on how they felt about crying. Saundy's husband, Jodean, died after a prolonged illness. She told me: "I find myself crying when I do something by myself that Jodean and I used to do together. For example, at church, he always sat in the middle of the 3rd row in front of the choir. He would smile at me as we sang. I would smile back and sing to him. Now when I look out from the choir loft, I notice his empty seat and I sometimes tear up. It helps to look elsewhere, contact, and smile at other congregants."

Carla shared, "The first year after my Dad died, I would cry when I was alone. Many times when I was driving home from work and saw the almond trees blooming, I would tear up because Dad always liked going for a drive when things were blooming. As a memento, I took some of his neckties to use as costume pieces for the theatre, and I would choke up a bit as I was putting them away after a show. He didn't wear neckties often as he got older, but he did dress up for church when we were kids and wore ties then. They were a special memory of him that often made me cry."

Bonnie said, "Mostly, I only cry when I am alone. I seem to switch into a social mode when others are around, which keeps my feelings and tears at bay. What triggers my tears can run the gamut. For example, a couple of days ago, I spotted a box of tissues on a shelf in the laundry room that have been there since before my husband died. I am pretty sure he bought them. Why I didn't notice them before, I have no idea. But seeing those tissues on the 3rd anniversary of his cancer diagnosis, when the whole nightmare began, brought me to tears. I didn't cry for long because I had to return to feeding the cats. The cat food is stored in the laundry room where the tissues were. It may seem small, but it still brought some tears." Bonnie also said, "What seems to set me off is when I feel like I am spinning my wheels, can't get what I want, or feel sick. It's as if not having a husband to share these minor annoyances with makes them feel like they are bigger or insurmountable challenges. In the end, I overcome the tears, but first, if I am alone, they are there. Not sobs, only tears. The tears come from feeling frustrated, sorry for myself, and alone—very alone."

Patti shared, "It would be accurate to call me a sentimentalist. I cry easily. Hearing the "Star Spangled Banner" and the "How Great Thou Art" hymn will often bring tears. Holiday commercials that emphasize a happy home life can make me cry. In relation to my parents—who are both dead for several years—the tears come at times, often unexpectedly. A movie coming on that Mom really liked might trigger tears. Realizing it is the date of their birth or death anniversary can catch me off guard with tears as well. On my recent trip to see fall colors, traveling a route I did with my dad, brought some tears. I shared the details of my mom's passing with a friend over lunch and cried a bit. I sometimes mist up if I see something that reminds me of either of my parents—a hummingbird, lilacs in bloom, a penny on the sidewalk waiting to be picked up. The tears are not overwhelming, not weeping. They are part of the unexpected memory—and then I move on with the day's activities."

If crying goes on for you longer than you can handle, you may consider seeking more professional support to help you in ways that may go deeper and be more therapeutic. If your loved one was taken from you in an accident, a suicide, or a violent crime, their untimely death could seem unbearable. You may be unable to eat, sleep, or get out of bed. You may be unable to stop some of the crying. If your crying becomes too difficult to handle, please get help. Start with who you are most comfortable with, like a close friend, a counselor, a minister, or a doctor. There is no shame in asking for help while grieving. We all will experience grief in our lifetime. The most important thing you can do is take care of yourself during the process.

PRACTICE: WALKING MEDITATION

I meditate every morning, sitting outside. When times get especially emotional for me, I find that if I do a walking meditation, I can clear my head and heart and take a deep breath again. To do a walking meditation, first, I find a beautiful, peaceful spot. I usually take my phone and earphones along and find a good meditation recording to play in the background, unless I am going to walk at the beach where I can't hear the music over the waves. Whether it is music or waves that accompany you, be sure they are relaxing background noise. Clear your mind and focus on your breath as you slowly walk. Notice all the beauty along the way as you settle yourself. Walk until you feel complete. You'll know when is the perfect time to end your walk, as your body will tell you. Listen to your body and how you are feeling, and follow its lead.

When you stop walking, take a few slow, deep breaths and express your gratitude for what you experienced. Try to incorporate a walking meditation into your practice at least once a week to help you to connect with your inner self and experience peace in your heart.

Key Tips for Chapter Six

1. Grief can pop up any time when you don't expect it.
2. Random triggers for grief can be expected.
3. When grief comes up, experience it, then move forward.

Take Action

HAPPINESS HABITS

Your Intention

*   Write an *Intention* to deal with your tears moving forward.

I intend to _____

_____

_____

_____

_____

_____

_____

_____

_____

Your Gratitude

* Write what you are *grateful* for in relation to tears that you have cried or are still crying.

I am happy and grateful that _____

_____

_____

_____

_____

Your Happiness

* In relation to what you read about tears, remember a time that you cried and how your tears ultimately brought you some *happiness*.

_____

_____

_____

_____

Your Affirmation

* Write a positive *affirmation* about the value of your tears.

I am _____

_____

_____

_____

_____

_____

_____

_____

CHAPTER 7
CHANGING YOUR SURROUNDINGS

"Change is the law of life. And those who look only to the past or present are certain to miss the future."
–JOHN F. KENNEDY

When my husband, Jacques, died, I realized I needed to sell our house. I had lived there for twenty-two years, and the house was too big for me alone. There was so much to care for, and I knew that being in that house would bring up constant memories. I found a much smaller house in a planned unit development where I didn't have to do yard work and keep the pool clean, and it was much closer to the university where I was teaching classes. Moving to a different house was a huge change, but I realized that was what I needed to do at that time for me to move forward and re-establish *my* life.

When a loved one transitions, your whole world seems to change, yet material things stay the same. The empty coffee mug that your husband had been drinking out of, your child's trophy collection, your mom's crochet project, or your friend's bicycle parked in front of your house sit there as if nothing has happened and are reminders that your loved one won't be touching these objects again. You may have shared your home with your loved one that is no longer there. In the case of a parent, friend, or adult child, your loved one may not have lived with you, but you may be involved in dealing with that person's belongings. All those 'things' can trigger your grieving.

Let's look at the ways that will serve you the most in dealing with the material things left behind. Instead of sorting through things as a dreaded task, use the opportunity to experience memories and to create a start for the new life you are beginning now.

I've known many people who could not face the idea of sorting through the belongings of a loved one. When my grandmother died, we ended up bringing all of grandma's possessions to my parents' house and stored them in their garage. We closed the door to the garage and didn't enter it for years. Years later, my mom finally allowed me to help her go through some of my grandmother's boxes. We discovered beautiful love letters my grandmother and her first husband had exchanged because he had to work thirty miles away from their home and she only saw him on weekends. He died very young because when he suffered from extreme stomach pain, he was put on a train to get to the closest hospital and his appendix ruptured along the way. The letters showed a side of my grandmother that my mother and I had never known. We also discovered letters my grandmother's brother had sent her from Hawaii when he was teaching close to Pearl Harbor during the war. The letters came after the bombing attack and were censored with words carefully cut out by the censors. Those letters were such a fascinating discovery.

You may be amazed by what you find as you go through the process of sorting what a loved one has left behind. Often, people keep a kind of shrine to their loved one who died, holding onto their possessions and things. They sometimes get a rental unit and put everything away to collect dust while paying a monthly fee. In the beginning, setting things aside to deal with later maybe the best you can do at the time. But instead of bringing comfort, not dealing with all the material things left behind for an extended period of time may drag out the pain of loss.

To support you in overcoming the pain material things can bring, you may want to consider doing some redecorating. Leaving things as they are can create a constant reminder of the past, of what you and your loved one had together. By changing things up, you can bring freshness to your world. Instead of living in the past, you can live in the *now* and look forward to a different future than you anticipated.

When my mom died, she left so much stuff that she knew my sister and I would want to remember her and my dad by. I had many boxes of newspaper clippings and programs of events. I know each piece of paper was very significant to her, but I remembered the whole of who Mom and Dad were. Keeping those many items was not going to help keep her memory alive in me. Both my parents were terrific servants to the community and did much for Veteran advocacy on the state and national levels. Those are the memories I cherish, not the things they left behind. Mom could never throw anything away, having lived through the depression. She had kept most of her clothes from the previous 50 years! And her pantry, what a mess. I was cleaning up outdated canned goods that had exploded in the pantry I don't know how many years ago! Going through the things in her home was both emotional and sentimental, but I realized that the material times were not what I needed to stay feeling connected to her.

When my husband, Ron, died, dealing with his 'things' was so different. We had moved from California to Maui two years before he transitioned. In that process, we released probably half of what we owned were all things that we didn't use. When Ron went on peritoneal dialysis, I had to find room in our house for all the required supplies, so I purged much more of the "stuff" we had. By the time he died, there was so much less to go through, and I was grateful. I realized that many things he had saved weren't things I wanted. When his children went through them, they left much behind. For instance, he had photo albums in which no one recognized the pictures, so we saw no reason to keep them. The albums were important to him, so letting them go was hard. He also brought a lot of art to our relationship. I was able to pass on the pieces that I did not enjoy as much to people who did, and that felt wonderful.

LETTING GO OF THINGS

What is the perfect time to sort things out? There is no perfect time, but I can guarantee that the longer you wait, the harder it is. You will never *really* be ready, so please don't wait for that. There are three ways to go through the process of releasing things. Only you can choose what works best for you.

* Your friends and family can come in and take away unneeded items right after the death.
* You can go slow and steady, committing to removing things systematically.
* You can leave everything the way it is until you are ready to release them.

If you choose to throw away, donate, or give away your loved one's clothes and possessions, chose a time you can dedicate your full focus to the task. You may want to ask a friend or two to help you. When you are ready, start with lots of big trash bags. Throwing things away is necessary, and it's okay. If you donate, take the time to decide which charities you would like to support or which organizations your loved one would have preferred. When it comes to giving, trust your instincts on who would appreciate what you wish to give away; that will aid the process. As you are sorting through items, designate where they will go (I am sure I stocked an entire bookstore for the *Friends of the Library*!). When you finish, deliver all of the items to their destination or arrange to have them picked up. The process of releasing these items will release the heaviness of the anticipation of sorting and emotionally getting rid of that weight.

A wonderful way to organize everything is to bring your family and friends together for a day or a weekend and have a plan. Decide what you want to accomplish. You may have your children go through boxes of saved items like photo albums or memorabilia. Check first to see if there is anything that you want to keep for yourself, then let them decide what they want and then release what is left to be donated or taken to the trash. Right after Ron died, we had family and friends gathered, so I went into Ron's closet and took out what I really wanted to keep, like his ministerial robes and the shirt by Nelson Mandela's designer I brought him from South Africa. Then the men went into his room, took what they wanted, and chose things to send to those who couldn't come to the house. I love knowing Ron's friends would be wearing his hat or shirt.

As family and friends work together to sort through belongings, you can support each other and reminisce on special memories, like, *Remember when she won that trophy?* Or, *Remember he wore that lucky hat to play golf?* Take the time you need to share celebrations and tears. Order your favorite food or turn on some music to set a more positive tone. Getting all the work done is not a race, so take the time you need. Remember that keeping too much stuff is a constant reminder of your loss.

As you review your loved one's material things, consider what you could repurpose. If your husband had a comfy shirt, *could you make a pillow with it?* If your mother had a fabric collection, *could you make a quilt with it?* If your child had a t-shirt connection, *could you sew your favorites together to make a little afghan you could put over your lap on cool evenings?* Since I love to sew, that's where my mind goes, but there are many other things you could do with your favorite things you'd like to keep from your loved one. When I had my theatre and school of arts, friends would bring theatre-related books to our library. People would also bring vintage or eccentric clothing to me for our costume department because they knew charities wouldn't appreciate those things like a theatre would. If you have a special initiative you support, consider what you can donate to them. Some ideas are:

* Books to *Friends of the Library*™
* *Dress for Success*™ for women's business clothes
* Battered Women's Shelter for women's and children's clothes
* *Habitat for Humanity Restore*™ for building materials
* *Boys and Girls Club*™ second-hand store furniture

When my husband, Jacques's, mother died, he put her house on the market and it sold within a week of the funeral. He was an only child, so the two of us were faced with rapidly emptying her lifetime's worth of belongings. She had many home decor items from the 1930s through the '50s. I used to borrow items from an antique store for props for my theatre, so I went to that store to ask if he'd like to come to see if he wanted any of the items. He took them all! I was thrilled to have him pack them up to take them away, and I was grateful to give him something he could use after all he had loaned to me. We also called extended family members to come to take what they wanted. We made a lot of people happy by giving her beloved items away.

MOVING PAST THE THINGS

Once you've had things cleaned out, *what do you do then?* Be willing to make some changes that will serve you. One of the best things I did after Ron died was to remodel our bathrooms. We had moved into our Maui home two years prior and had intended to remodel those outdated bathrooms, so it was a great place for me to start. I was able to put a deep soaking tub in the master bath and paint the walls using soothing, spa-like colors. My bathroom and tub have become my refuge, and I am grateful for my peaceful time there.

Ask yourself, *Where do you want to start?* You don't have to do big things; you can simply take it slow and choose those things that will help you feel better in your space. *What have you always wanted to do but never got around to?* Choose one item to change at a time and get started. Maybe begin with the room that will give you a precious space to relax, heal, and feel good in as you rediscover yourself.

You can start by painting walls or changing the curtains, pillows, comforters, and rugs. You don't have to do it all at once. Choose colors carefully depending on the feeling you want in a room. Years ago, a color study was done that showed that pink was a calming color, so many jail intake rooms and psychiatric facilities were painted pink, and the reports showed that color change was very effective. I chose colors that bring me comfort. I have always been drawn to warm colors, the colors of flames, like oranges, yellows, reds, and rich browns. While the rooms in my house are now painted a neutral color, the accents are mostly those warm colors. And my new bathrooms are painted a light turquoise, reminding me of the beautiful ocean waters nearby and bringing me the peace of a spa.

As part of your decorating, consider where to put pictures of your loved one that will comfort you. If your home is filled with many pictures, getting stuck in your past is easy, and moving forward is difficult. Choose pictures that are special to you and strategically place a few in places that will bring you pleasant memories. Try placing most of the pictures in a scrapbook you can look through when you are wanting more connection. Managing your pictures honors the memory of your loved one while allowing you breathing space during your emotional transition.

Sorting, cleaning, and redecorating are powerful ways to care for yourself. Find joy by sharing memories with friends who are helping, or writing special memories in a journal.

PRACTICE: CHANGING YOUR SURROUNDINGS

Now is a great time to plan a redecorating project or item purging process. Start by writing a list to prioritize what you want to do. I made my list by including rooms, cupboards, or even shelves I wanted to sort through and clean and rearrange as needed. I had been having to make many changes since we moved to Maui, relating to making space for Ron's medical needs, so when he was gone all of the equipment and boxes needed to go away also. I planned my efforts so that I did not become overwhelmed. Some days I could only do a drawer or a shelf, but I decided to celebrate the small milestones. Now my home is peaceful and comfortable. *What do you need to do to get to the place where your home is peaceful and comfortable?* Create a plan and get started. You can do it! I have faith in you.

KEY TIPS FOR CHAPTER SEVEN

* Make your special room yours by changing your decor.
* Discover what else you can change in your house to bring you joy and peace.
* Know that you can make any changes you want to.

TAKE ACTION

HAPPINESS HABITS

Your Intention

* Write an *Intention* about what you will do to change your surroundings, and set a time limit for when your changes will be complete.

I intend to _____

_____

_____

_____

_____

Your Gratitude

* Write what you are *grateful* for that you discovered in the process of changing your surroundings.

I am happy and grateful for _____

_____

_____

_____

_____

Your Happiness

* In relation to what you read about changing your surroundings, *what did you discover that made you happy that you can display to remind you of happy memories?*

_____

_____

_____

_____

_____

Your Affirmation

* Write a positive *affirmation* about what you are going to do to keep things in order now or only to keep things now that bring you sweet memories and happiness.

I am _____

_____

_____

_____

_____

_____

Chapter 8

Integrate Loss Into Your Life

"I've been to the water, and I've been baptized in pain and misery, but I just didn't feel like steppin' into it."

—MAMA BYARS

When you think about integrating loss into your life, a good place to start is to consider what your loved one would want for you right now. Ron and I had a discussion where he told me he had no idea how he could go on without me. Up to that point, I hadn't really thought of his perspective of how he would feel for him if I went first Since Jacques had died before I met Ron, I knew that I had persevered through that loss, but I didn't have a clear road map and stumbled through it. I asked Ron what he would want for me to do if he died first. In his sweet and caring way, he first said that he would want me to be happy. That wish was endearing and inspiring for me. When I would fall into the sadness or the tears that come with grief, I would think, *Would Ron want me to be sad? Would he expect me to cry so much?* Then I would take a deep breath and decide what my next step would be (even if it was to have a good cry), I would eventually pick myself up and carry on.

Through the use of my journaling, I decided to make a plan of things that I thought would help me move forward into my new normal. First on my list was to make a doctor's appointment—during Ron's diminishing health, my blood pressure had gone up, my heart rate became irregular, and my blood sugar was too high. To my surprise, my doctor took me off my medications when I attended my appointment. He explained that since I hadn't had my symptoms before Ron got so sick, chances are they had been caused by the stress I was going through. He had run all the appropriate tests before, so he had a good baseline of my health. I did as he said. I stopped all the drugs, and miraculously, my heart rate, rhythm, blood pressure, and blood sugar returned to normal.

Now is a great time to physically take care of yourself to feel your best. Get checked by a medical professional to ensure your health is optimal. See if there may be some medications you don't need to take or maybe some you do need. The body needs vital healing and support during the grieving phase.

While your focus is on your health, analyze your eating habits. While both my husbands were ill, I implemented their dialysis diet, which is not balanced or low in calories—so unsurprisingly, I gained weight in their last months of life. After they died, I didn't feel like eating at all, so I rapidly lost weight. I realized that I had to take care of myself to be healthy. I found that I felt much better when I was giving my body the proper fuel it needed. Eating a lot of snack foods and sweets and/or drinking carbonated sodas or alcohol may provide comfort and make you feel better temporarily; cutting those elements out of your diet is so much better for your restorative health.

The next important step is to seek out caring people. Generally, people you know care about you, but they may not know what to do or say while you are grieving. Help them out a little by communicating your needs. If you have friends and are not hearing from them, start by sending a text, email, or even a note in the mail. Tell them you miss them and suggest you get together for a cup of tea, a walk, a meal, or a movie night. Usually, friends want to connect, but they are unaware of the best way to reach out.

I had to fly to California on business and stopped by to spend a few days with my friend Rose while I was there. She lives in Ventura, the community we moved to Maui from. Rose hosted a potluck at her house while I was there and invited all the friends I knew. I loved our wonderful gathering that brought together so many friends I hadn't heard from since Ron died. They didn't know how to break the ice with me before Rose had a party. I found myself at the door all evening because people really wanted to talk to me when they came in. At the end of the evening, I hadn't gotten any of the lovely food from the potluck, but I was filled up with hugs, kisses, and love. Most of them have stayed in touch with me since then.

You may be saying to yourself, " I don't have any friends who want to deal with my loss." When Jacques was ill for two years, in and out of the hospital, he had many visitors at first, but by the time he died, people had stopped coming around. I felt lonely, so I thought of ways to reconnect with people. If there were an event, I would call people I had enjoyed doing things with and ask if they could give me a ride. That worked well and even led to some of them calling me to see if I wanted to go where they were going. Think of someone you know who would love the opportunity to go places with you for fun. Then extend an invitation and see what happens.

You can also find new friends who are dealing with grief by attending gatherings for the very purpose of helping people through the grieving process. See what support groups are available where you live. I discovered a *Death Cafe* in my town. A *Death Cafe* is a gathering of people who want to hold discussions regarding death. You can find a *Death Cafe* in many communities, and if you don't, you can start one. There is no agenda or objectives other than to support. Everyone has a chance to say something, and you can meet interesting people there. And, bonus—*they usually serve the cake.* Another thing that is becoming popular is a *Death Dinner Party*. These were started by the younger generation of 20 to 30-year-olds who were dealing with loss, but anyone could host one. By attending a group of people who are also grieving, I discovered that speaking to people who I don't know about my experiences made it easier to open up. I had no fear of judgment and met new friends with a common understanding.

It is also quite common for those experiencing grief to live in the past. There are some people I eventually had to distance myself from because they could not deal with the present and could not see there was a future. My mother had a hard time after my Dad died. She spent much of her time sitting without wanting to do anything except talk about the past. My sister and I knew what she was doing and did our best to love her through it. I didn't realize that I was doing a lot of focusing on the past until Ron pointed it out to me. He shared that he'd love to learn about the person I was then, unlike all I had done before he met me. That was a big wake-up call and helped me change my perspective.

Another way people deal with grief is to ignore it. They want to avoid it and not integrate it into their life. If you ignore it, it does not go away. Actually, it can grow, fester, and get worse. Facing your feelings and dealing with them can help you to move forward. Do things where you can incorporate your feelings into your life and feel good about mentioning your loved one's name. You'll find that when you smile when you say it, those around you will be able to smile, also. Talking about the person who died is perfectly natural, and those around you will take the cue from you to know you are comfortable speaking about it. They'll feel better about having the conversation, also.

Let's discuss the old myth that you must be strong when grieving. That was made up by someone who had not lost someone yet. Yes, there are times when you feel you need to keep it together, like when signing papers or giving a speech, but there are plenty of times when it is perfectly okay to shed tears. For me, apple pie brings waterworks. Apple pie was Ron's favorite dessert that he wanted for every occasion. Of course, I can also cry thinking about golf or pancakes. Everyone has triggers, and that's understandable. Sometimes triggers bring tears and feelings of frustration and anger. All of those are normal. Eventually, most triggers will bring a deeper meaning inside of you and conjure a smile of a personal unspoken secret.

Exercising is great because it gives you something to focus on and helps you feel better. I had a hard time first getting out of bed and then off the couch. During that time, I lost muscle tone, and I found it difficult to get up and move around, let alone actually exercise. But then there came a point for me when I realized that I had to get moving. Sitting around was not serving me, and if I ever wanted a better quality of life, I had to reach for it. I started by taking short walks around the neighborhood. At first, I wanted to talk myself out of them. Then I got a magic surprise in the mail. My insurance company was offering the opportunity to join a gym for free. I took that as a sign and enrolled. I bought an introductory training package and loved the help the trainer gave me. Since I didn't have to pay for the gym membership, I paid for the trainer. I have been going to the gym ever since, and I feel better and stronger every time, not to mention I sleep better. I also have been enjoying the beach and forest walks and making new friends to work out, walk, and hike with. I encourage you to get on up now and enjoy becoming stronger and exercising to benefit your health!

For those who belong to a church or participate in any kind of religious belief, now is a good time to go deeper. Seek sources within your faith, whether services, groups, counselors, or books. The advice and wisdom you discover will be supportive and beneficial. Lean into your faith during this time as you will find much comfort there. Seek out others who share your beliefs and find ways to support each other. Implement what you learn in ways that serve you and support your highest good

I found talking to my friends who were also dealing with loss helped to put things in perspective for me. When I asked them about their experiences of loss and how they deal with it, they had much to share. Bonnie, a life coach, said, "I feel loss all the time. In the beginning, after my husband died, loss felt like a missing limb. Now that loss feels more like a phantom limb. All the losses I have experienced (big and small) are part of my life story. They are not a unique chapter; rather, they are turning points in the plot of my story. Loss, even at its most painful, always helps me to see how alive I am." Consider Bonnie's words and ask yourself, *How alive do you feel right now? What can you do now to recognize your aliveness and help that feeling grow?*

My creative theatre friend Carla, who lost her father, said that she "Accepts that it is okay to miss my loved one, and it's okay to be sad that he is not here. I have things Dad made around the house so I can remember things that we shared. I don't dwell on his death but accept that it was part of what we share about him and is part of what makes us human. We appreciate each other more, knowing there will be an end." Use Carla's perspective to ask yourself, *What things do you have that you remember your loved one by?* I have some pictures on the walls and art that we bought together. I love to reminisce when I see those items, and they bring back good memories.

My trainer Ellis, who still grieves his mother, said, "I make sure I have the essence of her surrounding me. I ensure I *see* her name and *use* her name every day!" Ellis includes his mother's name in his email address and car license plate. *In what ways can you think of where you can use your loved one's name?* I include Ron's name in some form in my passwords, so I think of him every time I sign into my computer or my different accounts.

My friend Cathy said that she is adjusting to her new normal after losing her husband. "I need things done around the house that typically my husband would do. I am trying to do them myself, and that is a big step for me. Additionally, I have made new friends by finding people who can help me, and I am always pleased that they are happy to help." Get support from a trusted friend or financial advisor if you need to. Know that is okay to lean on others.

Annis, a talented poet who lost many friends, told me that she used her loss in writing poems and short stories. She allowed her feelings to influence her writing in a way that was carthic and healing. You may want to be inspired by Annis and begin writing a memoir, nonfictional account, or even a fun fictional story influenced by your loved one. Ask yourself, *What can you write about your loss that would help you remember and know how to move forward? What can you create in writing that will help you and also help someone else?*

Everyone has experienced loss in their lifetime. Sharing with others your experiences of grief shows you that you are not alone. Integrating that loss into your life instead of trying to overcome it helps you deal with it more effectively. Loss doesn't go away, but it does become an experience you have had in your life. When feelings of loss bubble up, experience them, appreciate them, and lovingly go on to the next experience. Those feelings and memories will still be there, but the intensity will fade and eventually become part of your life's beautiful blessed scenery.

PRACTICE: WRITING HAIKU POETRY

In the *Writing Though Your Grief* group I facilitate on Maui, one of our favorite exercises is to write Haiku poetry. Haiku is a Japanese poetry form that has only three lines. The first and third lines have five syllables each. The middle line has seven syllables. Initially, Haikus were written about nature and would incorporate some kind of surprise at the end. I encourage those in the group to consider what they would like to express in their poem, then write it however they want to. I encourage you to do the same. Write your own Haiku about what you are feeling. It is fine to have a couple more or fewer syllables than traditional Haikus because the most important thing is to express whatever you wish to express. You can have fun counting syllables on your fingers as you write. Here are a couple of examples:

Sitting alone now
Listening to the birds sing
His chair is empty

How I miss his touch
My lips ache for his kisses
My marvelous man

I can get through this
Strength is here with me always
Let me find my life

Write a few Haiku poems. You will be pleasantly surprised at what you come up with.

Key Tips for Chapter Eight

* Writing sweet memories you have of your loved ones in a Haiku helps you smile.
* Try writing positive poetry to lift your mood.
* Get outside in nature often.

Take Action

HAPPINESS HABITS

Your Intention

* Write an *Intention* about what you will do to spend more time with friends or to find new friends.

I intend to _____

_____

_____

_____

Your Gratitude

* Write who you are *grateful* to for being there for you while you are
  grieving. Include how each friend has helped or is helping you.

I am happy and grateful that _____

_____

_____

_____

_____

_____

Your Happiness

* Write about a *happy* experience you have had with someone else who is
  also dealing with grief and how you have been able to support each other.

_____

_____

_____

_____

_____

Your Affirmation

* Write a positive *affirmation* about something new you are
  integrating into your life to help you deal with grief.

I am _____

_____

_____

_____

_____

_____

_____

_____

_____

Chapter 9

Comparing Griefs

"Expand your inner capacity for radical empathy."
–JEAN HOUSTON

Everyone experiences grief in his or her own way and time. Some people go back to work after only a couple of days off. They may throw themselves into their career to avoid dealing with the emotions grief creates. Other people can't even bring themselves out of bed for an extended period of time. The key is not to judge your actions because your grief and how you cope with it is unique to you. It is natural to notice others who are grieving when we are grieving. We're in unfamiliar territory and looking for guideposts along the way, yet when we do, we tend to compare what we are feeling or how we are acting to what we observe in others. If you do find yourself comparing your journey, choose to observe instead and see what insight you can learn from that observation.

I saw a statistic that said at any given time, 90% of the planet's population is grieving someone, meaning that almost all of us are, at one time or another, feeling the effects of grieving. *Since so many of us are dealing with grief at some level, what can we learn from each other?* I believe sharing the process of grieving can assist in many ways.

Many of us may have been going about our lives, but then someone close to us dies, and a major paradigm shift occurs. Maybe, when your mother dies, you'll never be able to go to her for advice again or enjoy the Sunday dinner she so lovingly prepared for you every week. Maybe, when your partner dies suddenly in an accident, they are not there for your child's wedding or to sit outside with you to watch the sunset. Or when your spouse passes due to illness, and you are grateful that the pain and suffering are over for them. Or when your beloved pet dies, who has been your companion for many years, and you no longer cuddle up with them on your feet in the evening as you watch television. *Are these deaths comparable? Would you deal with each of them the same?* Of course not. At the same time, each death has drastically changed your life.

When you compare how you have reacted to the deaths in your life, you see that each one affected you differently. Think about how you would respond if your high school friend was killed in an accident, your grandmother died in her sleep, your good friend died after a long battle with cancer, your dog got hit by a car, your spouse died of a brain aneurysm, your favorite teacher died of pneumonia, your neighbor died of Covid. Take some time to consider who has died in your life. Then think about how you responded when deaths occurred in your best friend's or spouse's life. What is important here is to pay attention to how your life changes in relation to each loss. *What is different for you now? How can you best honor your loss while taking care of yourself?*

My office mate Patti, who has had both of her parents die, explains that she does not directly compare her loss to the losses others experienced. She knows that we each grieve in our own way and that grief takes its toll in different ways with each person. However, when observing those closest to her experiencing grief, she has not always understood others' feelings or their behavior. For example, she had had several friends lose their spouses. They were devastated, so overcome with tears and sadness, they could not function for several days. Patti has never been married, so she did not know what that sort of loss felt like. All she can do when others are dealing with loss is to try to be there and offer hugs, silence, a distraction, or maybe even some small treat like chocolate as comfort— whatever they need to help them take that next step forward.

GRIEF AND CAUSES

The *cause* of death often creates comparisons. When a drunk driver killed my friend's child, she received so much sympathy and support from the community, but when another friend was killed in an accident after he had been drinking, all the good he had done in his life was severely overshadowed by the circumstances surrounding his death. I heard such things as, "He deserved it when he was drinking and driving," "He should have known better," and, "What did he think would happen when he got behind the wheel drunk?" I was heartbroken that not only did I lose such a good friend who was a teacher, but his students also lost the knowledge and mentorship he so happily shared. His death, not his full life, was how others remembered him.

When someone you know dies, though the loss brings sadness, focusing on the gift of that person's life and sharing that with others is a gift that you can give to yourself. When my first pregnancy ended halfway through, my loss was completely different than when I lost my parents, my aunts and uncles, or my husbands. As each event occurred, I grieved the person for who they were and what they meant to me. Any one of those losses wasn't easier or harder than the other. My first pregnancy was not viable, and my mother-in-law lived into her nineties, but when or how they died was not significant—my love for them was.

The location where someone dies can also bring about comparisons. A dear friend of mine was devastated when she had a miscarriage that tragically happened in her bathroom toilet. When she heard that I had been in the hospital when I miscarried, she was mad at me and said it wasn't fair. Nothing is *fair* about having a miscarriage or suffering the death of someone you love. Later I dealt with more early miscarriages that suffered the same fate as hers, and I thought of her every time. My husband Jacques died as he sat down in our new car. He had a heart attack and slid between the seat and the dashboard. I couldn't do anything to help him. I struggled to get him out of that position to try CPR, but he was stuck. After he died, getting in that car became harder and harder for me, and I ended up selling it. Every time I looked in the direction of where he was trapped, the whole painful experience came rushing back.

The pandemic brought with it so many deaths in hospitals, which we traditionally have thought of as a place for healing. Many of us had loved ones in a hospital or a care home, and we were not allowed to see them. Lack of contact was devastating for so many people; for those who were ill and those who loved them. Our world has changed so much with the pandemic. In many ways, most of us are kinder and gentler to each other, while others have stayed angry.

Specific locations can bring memories that haunt us. On one stretch of highway that I regularly traveled, I knew right where my friend had run head-on into a semi-truck and died and where one of my students stopped on that highway at a stoplight when a large truck ran into her car, killing her instantly. I could not avoid traveling on that road as it was the only one that took me where I needed to go. To this day, when I travel past the last places they were, I can't help but think of them. My husband, Ron, passed peacefully in our home, surrounded by family and friends. I have no problem with where he transitioned because the circumstances differed. Where death occurs doesn't really matter in the long run, so comparing where your loved one's death occurred, as opposed to where someone else died, doesn't serve a purpose.

How someone dies is another matter. When someone dies a violent death, the comparison comes when the griever compares what could have been done differently. *If only they hadn't gone out with his friends that night. If only he didn't go swimming where he knew it was dangerous. If only they hadn't started hanging out with those who were always in trouble. If only she had moved out when he started getting violent. If only people wouldn't drive when they have been drinking.* Comparing what *could have, would have, and should have* happened does not help. I had two friends commit suicide a month apart. I compared those deaths for a long time, trying to figure out if I could have done something differently that would have made them reconsider. All that comparing did was keep me tied up in my feelings until I realized that there was nothing I could have done and that their suicides were not about me.

Knowing How to Say Goodbye

When we start comparing deaths, we start questioning our decisions. My friend Carla's father had never mentioned what he wanted when he died. She knew her father would have appreciated what she did for his memorial service, but when his friend died and had a big funeral, it caused Carla to wonder if she had done the right thing; if her dad had actually wanted something similar. It was too late to change his funeral, but she knew her dad was a proud veteran, so she could have a memorial stone put in for him at the national cemetery close to where he had lived, which helped her be more at peace.

I am grateful that in the case of my husbands and my parents, I had discussions with them before they died, so I knew exactly what they wanted. Their wants were all so different, so I appreciated their guidance. My parents' funerals were huge, Jacques' funeral was very big, and Ron had two services: one in Maui with a traditional Hawaiian ash scattering in the ocean and the second one at *Agape International Spiritual Center,* where his good friend Rev. Michael Beckwith was able to facilitate with his friends and family who lived on the mainland. Some people don't care what happens after they die, and some people desire to be remembered in a certain way. How a celebration of life is handled is a personal decision and any decision made for handling things is perfect, with no room for comparison or judgment.

Grief coach, Bonnie, calls these comparisons the 'Grief Olympics.' When she went to a support group and sat next to a young widow with three children under five, she felt she should keep quiet about her loss since the other woman had it *so* much worse. However, she soon realized that her feelings were hers and that she had the right to embrace them.

While my trainer, Ellis, says that he never compares grief because no one could ever feel the pain of losing his mother, my friend, Cathy, said she ended up comparing her loss to the loss of a friend whose husband died, leaving her with two young children. When that happened, Cathy was grateful that she had so much time with her husband before he died, and she only had to deal with her grief, not the grief of any children.

When you look at all the examples in the chapter, I can hear you saying, *but it's not the same. My grief is different. My grief is the worst. I'm too young to experience grief. I'm too old to live without my spouse. I am not equipped to help my children grieve.* I want you to realize that comparing yourself to others will not serve you. Everyone has a unique experience. The word unique means *one of its kind,* unlike *anything* else.

Sometimes, people can say something they don't realize is hurtful or insensitive. I had one person say she knew how I felt when my second husband passed because her dog had died. I know that many people think of their animals as their children, but comparing her dog to my husband did not feel comparable to me. When I had my miscarriage, several people said it was okay because I could always have another child. They did not know that I had been an infertility patient for three years and that another child might not happen. I don't hold these misspoken words against someone who genuinely is trying to offer comfort in their own way, but I do find that I try my hardest not to say something to someone who is grieving that will only make things worse.

When I had my miscarriage, I felt like I was dealing with it alone. My husband found reasons not to spend time at home, and we didn't discuss what had happened. I decided he didn't know how I felt and thought I was making a big deal over nothing. Years later, he finally decided to tell me that he hadn't been spending time with me or talking to me then because he was grieving. He didn't know what to say or do, and he was so sad that he was afraid he would make me sadder instead of being able to help me. I felt terrible and selfish when he told me his feelings. I wish I could have been able to do something different at the time. I see now that I was unconsciously comparing our losses, which hurt us both.

In every case, when someone dies, you will grieve in your own way and in your own time. You may feel regrets, have needs, long for your loved one, feel guilty, or be so stressed that you don't know what to do. Whatever the case, you must deal with it in your own way with grace and vital self-care.

My aunt and uncle were good friends with another couple. Both couples had spent much time together and knew each other well. They were elderly. My family judged my uncle harshly when he married the wife of the other couple shortly after my aunt and her husband died. I believe it was a beautiful opportunity for them both to aid each other's loneliness and celebrate their loved ones who were no longer there.

There are no winners in the 'Grief Olympics.' Try not to compare; instead, release judgment and practice love.

PRACTICE: MINDFULNESS

Comparing our experiences to the experiences of others can bring on added anxiety or confusion as we think of what other grievers are feeling. The best way to deal with comparing is to practice mindfulness. When you center yourself on the present moment, not thinking about the past or wondering about the future, you are being mindful. Paying attention to our thoughts is especially important when grieving because falling into depression and pain can dominate how you feel when you focus on your loved one who died and all the experiences around that. Grievers tend to think of all they no longer have when focusing on the future. However, when you focus on what you do have right now, you can experience happiness and discover what is best for you currently.

Here are some simple ways to practice mindfulness:

* **Breathe:** Take time to be still and focus on your breath. Practice taking slow, deep breaths, concentrating on how your body relaxes and how good it feels to breathe.
* **Acceptance:** Know that right now, all is well. Release thinking about anything that is not in your control.
* **Compassion:** Genuinely connect with others mending any hard feelings and supporting them emotionally as they deal with problems.
* **Emotions:** Pay attention to your emotions. When they intensify, think about if the feeling you are experiencing serves you and if they don't, focus on creating a positive emotion instead.
* **Eat:** Eating mindfully helps you to maintain a healthy weight. Take time to enjoy what you are eating and choose only healthy foods.
* **Sleep:** Get an appropriate amount of rest for you. Go to bed at the same time and rise at the same time. Start and end your day with a peaceful practice like journaling or prayers.
* **Walk:** Take time every day to walk outside, enjoying the beauty you see, from clouds to the blue sky to flowers and all the nature around you. Enjoy how your muscles feel as you move and breathe outdoors.
* **Gratitude:** The more you are grateful, the more you will see what you have to be grateful for. Write your gratitude in a journal. Express your gratitude to those who are kind to you.
* **Listen:** When someone is speaking, focus on what they are saying rather than thinking about how you want to respond.
* **Thinking:** Pay attention to what you think. Focus on positive thoughts and the beauty that surrounds you.

There are endless other ways to be mindful. Incorporate mindfulness practices into your daily life. Practice staying in the present moment. The more you focus on the present, the more mindful you will be.

KEY TIPS FOR CHAPTER NINE

* Everyone practices grief in their own way. Find the way that works for you.
* There is no particular time that grief takes. Take all the time you need.
* Every grief is different. Yours is personal to you.

TAKE ACTION

HAPPINESS HABITS

Your Intention

* Write an *Intention* about remembering that each loss is unique and how you can best support those grieving.

I intend to _____

_____

_____

_____

Your Gratitude

* Write what you are *grateful* for related to each loss you experience.

I am happy and grateful that _____

_____

_____

_____

Your Happiness

* In relation to what you read about comparing griefs, *what are you anticipating will bring you happiness as you move forward in dealing with your grief?*

_____

_____

_____

_____

_____

Your Affirmation

* Considering all the experiences you thought about as you read about comparing griefs, write a *positive affirmation* about one thing you would like to do to prepare for your own passing that will bring you peace of mind.

I am _____

_____

_____

_____

_____

_____

Chapter 10

Being Kind to Yourself

"Be kind to yourself and others. Come from love
every moment you can."
—DEEPAK CHOPRA

Being kind is part of my nature. I have always seemed to put everyone else first before myself. I've made sure everyone is fed, including the pets, before I eat. I defer to doing what others want instead of standing up for my desires. I open the door for a stranger. All these things are good, but I saw that others often did not consider me. I had to make myself important. When I started taking care of myself, it allowed me to integrate my loved one's death into my heart and soul in a way that wasn't overshadowed by my need to help everyone else.

When you are in the middle of deep loss, what my sculptor friend, Maryann, calls "total-grief-meltdown-into-giant-puddle-of-tears-on-the-ground-days," chances are the last thing on your mind is taking care of yourself. But you must. You are the keeper of your body, heart, and soul; only you can tend to it best. If you haven't started paying attention to yourself, now is the time to start. If you have started, now is the time to ramp up your self-care initiative.

How do you be kind to yourself? Begin by focusing on your body, heart, mind, and soul. Each one of these parts of you needs care and compassion. Keeping them in balance is the key to recovering your joy. Compassion is generally defined as a deep feeling of sympathy and sadness. Compassion also means a passion for living and life. We often need to show ourselves compassion and feel renewed passion. Now is the time to care for all parts of you passionately.

YOUR BODY

Your body physically responds to the trauma from the death of a loved one. When the death is sudden, the effects will be different than when the death has been long awaited. How well you are prepared for death to arrive can help with the physical response, yet you can't fully escape that response. Symptoms that arise range from difficulty sleeping, sleeping too much, high blood pressure, racing pulse, headaches, ulcers, changes in appetite, low energy, and diarrhea. Not a pretty picture, as your body will react in unpredictable ways. Get help when you need to on any of these issues. There may be a quick way to get some relief that a doctor can provide by using your mindfulness practice to support you. When my husband Jacques died, I didn't sleep at all; when I did, I had nightmares. I finally got a prescription and got some much-needed sleep. I took the prescription for way too long, and it was hard to stop taking them. When my husband Ron died, I asked for the same prescription, but I only took it briefly. After that, I switched to something over the counter, and I was able to stop easily.

When you end up with symptoms of something physical that hinder your recovery, seek professional assistance. I did end up with many symptoms, and I sought help in various ways. I now have a wonderful acupuncture practitioner, a homeopathic doctor, a physician, and a personal trainer. I found it difficult to exercise on my own, so I joined a gym. I found a trainer who paid attention to me, allowing me to gain strength and energy through what he had me do each week, and my loyalty to him gets me to the gym. Ellis, my trainer, says: "The one thing in life that's free is exercise. That has helped me so much with everyday life and grief!"

Another great way to care for your body is to pamper yourself. A good massage therapist can help to release the tension and sorrow that builds up in your body—helping you to relax. Not talking during a massage makes a huge difference, so if you get a chatty therapist, find someone else. If you aren't used to getting massages, allow yourself the luscious indulgence. Get naked. Your privacy is always respected, and your therapist has seen more than you imagine and won't be surprised or affected by anything you might be concerned with. The importance of skin-to-skin touch is vital. When newborn babies aren't allowed enough touch, they develop a condition called "failure to thrive." Allowing yourself a good massage is allowing yourself to start to thrive again.

YOUR HEART

We often say our "heart breaks" when someone dies, and though that isn't an actual physical description, it feels like the truth. Handle your heart gently as you move forward. Find a place where you can feel the love all around and spend time there. Ron and I sat on our lanai (deck) daily. We had long conversations, watched and listened to the birds, and enjoyed the peace. Now every morning, friends join me to read and meditate. My mom used to say, "It does my heart good," and it certainly does my heart good as I sit there remembering Ron and Mom.

Ron and I would go to a place called The Sacred Garden, where we would meditate on the lovely labyrinth or sit in front of a huge, beautiful Buddha. I can go there now and still feel him with me. I also love our bed and bedroom, which we considered a sacred space. I know I will always find comfort there. *Where do you find comfort? Where is a place you can go and sit quietly and place your hand over your heart and whisper, "I've got you?"*

Another thing you can do for your heart is listen to music. Jacques taught me an appreciation for classical music, especially Baroque, J.S. Bach, and Mozart. Ron taught me an appreciation for Jazz, and I've always loved many music types. Now I am gaining an appreciation for the love and beauty of Hawaiian music. *What's your favorite music? Favorite song? What memories do different types of music or songs bring to you?* Surrounding yourself with music can do your heart good. I am listening to Bach's Cello Suite 1 in G major as I am writing this book, recalling the beautiful memories Jacques and I had from the Carmel Bach Festival. Turn on your music to accompany you through your day, or better yet, go to a concert!

Bonnie, a widow, shared, "I treat myself to little gifts. Nothing expensive. Most are little rewards for acknowledging when I do well. When I have challenging days, I show myself the same type of kindness. Usually, it's more in terms of something comforting." Annis, a poet, says: "I amp up the personal care: massage, facial, mani-pedi appointments. I remind myself that I'm human and it's okay to feel the feelings or not 'be over it'." Carla, whose father died, takes a hot bath with a good book. Or she goes for a walk on the beach. Peter shared that he devoted one day a week to going fishing and one weekend a month to going out in the wilderness to connect with nature.

Your Mind

Early when dealing with your loss, you can feel like your thoughts are working against you. I couldn't remember things. I felt like I was in a fog, not seeing, hearing, or caring about anything around me. I felt hollow. I couldn't smile. I couldn't read, which had been one of my favorite things to do. I sometimes turned the television on, but what was on didn't register with me. Finally, I started coming back to life. Slowly. Gradually. Moving out of these distracted thoughts took much longer after Jacques passed. After all, I'd been married to him for 22 years, and his transition was the first I had experienced so intensely. I was better prepared when Ron died, not because I had been through it before, but because I had changed so much mentally when it came to grieving. I had learned to live in a place of unconditional love with complete forgiveness, integrity, and mindfulness. Despite having those skills, getting through those early days and months took time and effort.

As I rose out of that fog, my biggest challenge was discovering what I was supposed to do next. My monkey mind, which Eckhart Tolle refers to as 'the voice in your head,' ran rampant, trying to convince me of doom, gloom, and purposelessness. Fortunately, I was familiar with that voice, and when it got especially loud, I would encourage it to take a break so I could meditate or write. Once I started writing, I found my voice and worked on any issues that came up by writing them down. As always, the more I shared my story, the less I had to dwell on it, allowing me to start fresh.

For you, now is the point where you start exploring what's next? Try journaling to discover what your real wants, needs, hopes, and wishes are. Take your time. Really explore yourself. You may discover that you want to change your career path. You may want to change your appearance, cut your hair or grow it out, lose weight, or gain some. Or you may want to travel or reconnect with old friends. There is no rush. Treat yourself gently with no pressure. Exactly what is supposed to happen will come to you when you are ready.

YOUR ACTIVITIES

Your activities up till now may have been centered around your loved one who isn't there to do them with you anymore. That may make doing anything new seem daunting at first, but you can do it! Take the time to encourage yourself to bring activities back into your life. How you take care of yourself now and your actions will help you heal. *What do you want to do?* Here are a few options to inspire you:

* **Take classes.** There are so many wonderful classes you can take online or in person. Contact your local community center and see their classes in various subjects. Consider drawing, watercolors, jewelry design, printmaking, glass blowing, or ceramics classes. Get lost in your creativity.

* **Travel.** Getting out and seeing new places will awaken and allow you to form different perspectives. Enjoy new foods and explore different cultures and their activities

* **Entertain.** Instead of waiting for someone to get you to go somewhere, invite your friends to do something with you.

* **Explore.** Take the time to discover beautiful places, go on gentle hikes, explore different beaches, botanical gardens, try whale-watching, or find great places to eat.

* **Create something.** Try something new. *What have you always wanted to create?* It can be anything from a vegetable garden, to a charcuterie board, to a bookcase. If you don't know how to create what you want, take a class or watch YouTube™ videos. You can find inspiration there!

YOUR SOUL

You may consider your soul to be your essence, who you are beyond your physical body. Your soul is filled with your emotions, beliefs, knowledge, and experiences. Our souls are where our approach to spirituality resides, ranging from Atheism to devoutly following a specific religion. Your approach doesn't matter as much as that you honor it.

I created a daily practice to nurture my soul based on what is important to me. Some people may visit their place of worship and find comfort there. Others may want to make a little altar somewhere in their homes or yards where they can visit with their loved ones. Maybe it's a special picture of you and them together. I have a couple of pictures I can't pass without smiling at them and kissing them.

If there is a burial spot, go there and be with your feelings. We scattered Ron's ashes in the ocean off Sugar Beach. We went out in an outrigger canoe and took turns scattering ashes and flowers. I now love to take walks on that beach where coincidentally, Ron and I went on our honeymoon. Find a place where you feel connected to your loved one and spend time there

If you pray, mention the name of your loved one. Always speak their name. Saying their name can be so comforting to you. Avoiding a name is like avoiding remembering a life filled with experiences and love. Speak directly to them. After my friend Cathy's husband passed, she told me, "I now walk around the house and talk to my husband; I laugh at things he would have thought funny or be mad at what would have disturbed him, so he is still part of my life."

Be kind to yourself. *What do you want? What do you need?* Whatever it is, do it. Know that you are doing the very best you can and being the very best you can be. Love yourself up. Rub off some of that love on others around you. Enjoy!

PRACTICE: BE KIND TO YOU!

Setting intentions is a great way to start taking care of yourself. You have created a new Happiness Habit by writing an intention at the end of each chapter. Take some time now to go through the intentions you have written so far. *Did you complete some of the things you set your intention for?* Congratulate yourself on a job well done! Then write another intention related to the ones you completed. Writing intentions is a great way to get you centered and moving forward. Commit to starting and continuing each new intention to care for your beautiful self!

KEY TIPS FOR CHAPTER 10

* Determine what you actually need.
* Determine what you actually want.
* Discover how meeting your needs and wants can lead you to live your best life.

TAKE ACTION

HAPPINESS HABITS

Your Intention

* Set an *Intention* to start one thing for each section of this chapter: body, heart, mind, activities, and soul. Write your intentions and read them daily as you get into the habit of doing them.

I intend to _____

_____

_____

_____

Your Gratitude

* Write what you are *grateful* for about the intentions you have fulfilled so far.

I am happy and grateful that _____

_____

_____

_____

_____

Your Happiness

* In relation to what you read about being kind to yourself, write a list of things you do to take care of yourself that make you *happy*.

_____

_____

_____

_____

Your Affirmation

* Write a *positive affirmation* about your favorite thing you do or want to do to assure your happiness.

I am _____

_____

_____

_____

_____

PERSONAL NOTES

CHAPTER 11
PUTTING YOUR AFFAIRS IN ORDER

"Peace is always beautiful."
–WALT WHITMAN

Hopefully, all of your financial affairs are in order. If not, that's okay, as this chapter will help you make some decisions and take action toward managing your important affairs. I am not an accountant or an attorney, but I have experience dealing with financial and legal issues when someone dies, I can tell you some of what needs to be addressed and who you can turn to for help. The tasks that must be taken care of may seem insurmountable, but they are not. Start by creating a document with a list of all your accounts, policies, and legal documents so you can follow your finances' trail. Also, be sure you have all the passwords you need and keep them secure. Get help if you can, but be careful who you get help from. Not everyone is ethical, and some may take advantage of you. Do your homework and ask others you trust who provide good services.

If you are dealing with a death, most of these will require a certified copy of the death certificate. Be sure to cancel any credit cards in your spouse's name only and put only your name on the cards you shared. Also, put your name on the deed if you own property, like your home. You may want to put one of your children as a signer on your bank account so that you can always access your money if something happens to you. This also applies to ailing parents or adult children you may be caring for.

Go through all the regular payments you make, and be sure you note down reminders of the due dates for payments. Often, one person in a couple handles all the bill paying, and if that person in your relationship was your spouse, this is extremely important for you to get on top of now to keep your financial affairs in order. It is easy to let payments slip or accidentally overdraw an account when dealing with trying times. These things will bring you stress and pressure at a time when you don't need more turmoil. It is important to be organized. You may want someone to help you stay on top of all your finances, especially making deposits and paying bills. You will find a sense of security when you know that everything is in order and you have told whoever you designated for these tasks that you are asking for their help if need be.

Be sure to update your will and any trusts you may have—and be sure you have your own power of attorney naming who will take care of you if the need arises and have a Durable Power of Attorney for Health Care naming who you want to make medical decisions if you can't. And be sure to tell the person you designate what you want. My Aunt Ila named me as her decision-maker but didn't tell me. Years later, her sister, another aunt of mine, was killed in a car accident. At the meal after the funeral, my aunt decided she better let me know that she had named me her decision-maker.

Make a Plan That Will Support You

When Ron started having severe health problems, we went to an attorney in California to be sure our legal affairs were in order. We were sure to get a Durable Power of Attorney for Health Care because I knew he did not want to be resuscitated if his heart stopped and he stopped breathing. Then we moved out of California and relocated to Hawaii. Two years later, when we set him up in hospice, they asked me for his DNR (Do Not Resuscitate) certificate. I handed them what I had, and they said that wouldn't do. I explained that it was completed, legal, signed, and certified as it needed to be. Still, they said that in Hawaii, it needed to be a single sheet with specific wording on a sheet of green paper that needed to hang on the refrigerator door! I am grateful they told me in time for me to be able to get the green sheet taken care of before an emergency services person took it upon themselves to start CPR on someone who didn't want it.

After someone dies, there can be lots of drama over who gets what. Of course, the best plan of action is for everyone to know the answers to that question ahead of time which can be taken care of with a will. I was fortunate that there was no problem either time. When Jacques died, I am afraid I gave his children way more stuff than they ever wanted to deal with, but I wanted the decisions of what to do to be theirs. Now I am working on lightening my load, giving things away, or letting people know what theirs will be when I am gone. No one will have to clean up after me. I did that for my mother and aunt, and it was not easy. Your loved ones will appreciate you so much if they don't have to deal with all the possessions and neglected legal concerns.

Take time to organize all your financial and legal affairs. Get help from professionals when you need to. Let your family or someone you trust know what they need to know about your affairs. Doing all this will bring you peace of mind.

PRACTICE: FINDING PEACE OF MIND

Great peace can come from having all of your affairs in order. Twice in my life so far, I have had to take over the responsibility for a loved one. I didn't know that this would be happening either time, so I didn't have the opportunity to work with either person while they could tell me what they wanted and what needed to be done. I promised myself I would not leave anyone in that position.

The practice for this chapter helps you to start getting organized so you know your loved ones will have access to everything they need related to you when the time comes. This information will be important if you aren't able to speak for yourself, and much of it is essential when you die. I suggest that you start with this list to have an idea of what you need. You may also want to go through this process with anyone you may be helping with their needs. Find a safe and secure place to store this information as you gather it.

1. Record all your personal details like your legal full name, birth date, place of birth, parents' full names, and their date of death.

2. Where are your birth and marriage certificates and divorce documentation located?

3. Your social security number, address, phone number, and email address.

4. Your retirement information.

5. Your driver's license number and your passport number.

6. Are you an organ donor? Are there specific organs you do or do not wish to donate?

7. Do you have a will? If so, who is your executor? Does this person know they have been designated as such? Do you have a Durable Power of Attorney? Do you have an Advanced Directive? Are all these documents and any other necessary documents legal and up to date? Who is your attorney?

8. Where are all your legal documents located, like the deed to your home and all other documents?

9. Have you designated a decision-maker? Does this person know your wishes? What is this person's name and contact information?

10. Do you have a written health history, including your blood type and the medications you are taking?

11. What current health conditions are you being treated for?

12. Who are your doctors, and what is their contact information?

13. What are your financial obligations? Where do you bank? What are your account numbers?

14. What health or life insurance policies do you have? What investments do you have?

15. Have you made funeral arrangements? If so, with whom? What is the contact information?

16. Where are any passwords you have located? Do you have a safety deposit box? Where is it located?

17. What are the names and contact information of all your accountants, gardeners, cleaning services, auto payments, charity donations, and any other service people you regularly deal with?

18. Have you designated arrangements for minor children or pets?

This is just a start. The more up-to-date information you have ready, the easier it will be for all involved.

KEY TIPS FOR CHAPTER ELEVEN

* Put your financial affairs in order.
* Update your legal documents.
* Develop a system to pay your bills and keep your documents in a safe place.

TAKE ACTION

HAPPINESS HABITS

Your Intention

* Write one *Intention* about something you will do to ensure your affairs are in order.

I intend to _____

_____

_____

_____

_____

_____

_____

Your Gratitude

* Be *grateful* for at least three things, like writing your will or completing a Durable Power of Attorney for Health Care, you have done so far to get your affairs in order.

I am happy and grateful that _____

_____

_____

_____

_____

Your Happiness

* Write what you will be happy about when you have your affairs in order. Reading your list will help you to see how important taking care of your affairs is.

_____

_____

_____

_____

_____

Your Affirmation

* Write a *positive affirmation* about how strong you feel when you take care of your business.

I am _____

_____

_____

_____

_____

_____

_____

CHAPTER 12
CREATING A VISION BOARD

"My creative process produces excellence and wholeness in all that I do, knowing that this is what returns to me a thousand times over."
–REV. RON THREATT

Chances are you have created a vision board, which some people call a dream board, at some point in your life. Since your life has changed so much by losing your loved one, now is the perfect time to create a new board, focusing on your future. Take a moment to think about your life as it is right now. *Have your goals changed? Do you know what direction you want to go? Are you doing what you really want to do? What is your life's purpose? How do you want your future to unfold?* Your vision board can help you answer all the questions and constantly remind you what you want to create going forward. Your mind responds to pictures, so having a visual image of your intentions can help your mind align with what you intend.

I made my first vision board after I met Ron. He had his vision board on the wall right in front of his desk. He didn't have to tell me what it was because I could clearly see it was his life. He saw it every day as a reminder of the joy he had in his life and the direction he was moving in. I decided I wanted that for myself. I was ready to focus on the life I had only dreamed of before, so I created my own vision of the future. On my board, I depicted a plan for living on purpose and realized that up to that point, though I did have some goals, I was more floating through life, completing my to-do lists without really contemplating what I wanted. Now, my vision board shows *my* vision. Through the process of creating my board, I had the advantage of talking with Ron as he was still alive. Every time we talked, I would gain inspiration for my board and add something meaningful. My board is a representation of the life I want and am moving into. It keeps me both grounded and focused on the future I can manifest.

MAKING A VISION BOARD

Before you start making your board, reflect on what you have accomplished already. Since your loved one is no longer with you, *what is new and different in your life? What is different about the intentions you have now? What changes do you want or need to make in your life to be in alignment with your ultimate intentions?* To help with your vision board creation, write an intention that fortifies how you feel and that you can frequently repeat as needed, like "I intend to live my best life at all times and in all circumstances." When you say something strong and positive, especially when your strength may start to falter, you bring yourself back up!

To create your vision, ask yourself what you want for your life and write what you see. First, read back through all the intentions you have written. Your intentions will provide you with a wealth of information to get started. Then, answer these questions, remembering that your answer should serve you best. Be creative. Think big. Know that you can have anything you want. Clearly state the intentions that you want to focus on.

1. *What do you need in life? What is most important to your personal survival?*
2. *What do you want in life? Dream big here. Is there a job or career you have always wanted? Is there someplace you have always wanted to travel? Is there someone or some group you have always wanted to serve?*
3. *What do you value? Are material items important to you? Are relationships important to you? How about fame or service or peace or rest?*
4. *What do you want to change? Your residence? Your weight? Your emotions? Your health?*

5. *What would you do if nothing was holding you back?* We often don't consider things because we don't have the time, money, or support to do them. Let go of all that and consider what you would really love to do!

6. *What is the most important thing you would really love to experience?* Be clear with your priorities before you search for the pictures for your board.

7. Consider not only what you need for your desires to manifest but also what you need to let go of so there is room for your manifestation to occur.

After you have answered these questions, think about what images would reflect what thoughts you came up with. *Where can you find these images?* If you have magazines, start looking for images there. Your friends may have magazines they'd love to pass along. You can do internet searches for the images you want to use. For instance, if you want to go to Bali, Google Bali, then click on images. There will be a wealth of images to choose from. Copy and print what you want to use that represents your ideas. Printing images takes lots of ink, so be judicious in your chosen ones.

Search for images that represent the high points of the answers to the questions you wrote. Be sure to have at least one iconic image for each important point. You also can include pictures of you, preferably smiling and joyful! Gather all your images and keep them in a folder or an envelope while you collect the rest of your pictures. You can also find words and phrases that express your intentions and cut them out to add to your board. Choose inspiring words that represent the feelings you most want to experience.

Decide what kind of surface you want to use to have a vision board that lasts. Get creative here and think about where you plan to place your board when it is complete. You may simply use a piece of poster board. Foam core board is a good choice because it is lightweight, available in various sizes, and sturdy. To get creative, use a wooden board, maybe repurposed for other use. Or get a piece of acoustic tile, cover it with fabric, and pin your pictures to it. Another idea would be to get a garage sale item like a framed painting, table, or desk and decoupage your pictures to it. There is no limit to your creativity here. Choose a method that most resonates with you.

Then gather what you will need to adhere to what you have collected to your board. Glue sticks work well to attach paper items, but you could also use picture mounting corners, pins, decoupage, paste, or you could even sew them on. Also, use items like colored pens, felt markers, glitter, sticky-back gems, and paint; anything you want to decorate your board with. There are multiple items at crafts stores and scrap-making shops if you really want to get fancy.

Find a space where you can put your board together. Be sure it's somewhere you won't mind having a bit of a mess for a while, as you may choose to take a couple of days to complete your project. Putting some plastic or an old sheet over the table is a good idea to avoid damaging it. Then do something to make the space inviting for you to work there. Bring some flowers in from the garden, light some incense, or put your favorite scented oil in your diffuser. Put some music on, preferably something calm, beautiful, and without words to distract you.

When you are all set up, take some time to meditate. Meditation will allow you to relax. Focus on seeing where your primary intention leads you. Say a prayer or ask for guidance from whoever or whatever you believe in. Then it is time to get started. The process of creating a vision board takes time. Remember that the more you put into it, as with anything, the more you will get out of it. Take all the time you need.

Spread out all the images you have gathered. Arrange them on your board before you do any attaching. Be sure to use a reasonable number of pictures and words. If you have lots of pictures and words, focusing clearly on your intention will be more difficult, so be sure to choose the things you desire the most. Save any items you don't use; you may want to create another board later to focus on new intentions—you may want to create more than one board; for instance, you may want one for your home life and one for your work life. When you are happy with what you have chosen and where you placed it, start attaching. You may want to frame it by putting a bigger piece of colored paper or fabric underneath it. Be sure to leave room for the words or phrases you have collected that you want to write on your board. Then add your words or phrases. You may want to decorate your board with ribbons or other items to make it beautiful and resonate with your intent. Write the date on your board to help you reflect on how far you have come with your intentions. Then, ta-da! You are done! Be sure to put on your calendar the date a year from the day you created your board to create a new board for your new intentions!

Now find a place of honor where you can put it. Put it where you can see it daily if you would like, or you can put it away knowing the work is already done by setting your intention when creating the board. Be sure to journal about the process. *What did you learn or experience by making your creation?* Know that the focus you have placed on your intention ensures that you see the results of that intention. Include in your journal what you recognize you are doing to support your intention. Each step you take helps manifest your intention, and your results become evident.

SET INTENTIONS FOR YOUR BOARD

When working on your intentions, remember that you are creating them for yourself. No one can create them for you. You need to do this work and be willing to discover about your life, future, and desired next steps.

Here are some suggestions you can do to activate your board and bring the future you desire closer to becoming your new reality:

* State your intentions in the present tense as they are happening now. When you state your intentions in the future, you may miss the opportunity to realize them now.

* Repeat your intentions out loud every day and smile while saying them.

* Look at your board every day, noticing the details and reminding yourself of your intent.

* Recognize when the results of your intentions become part of your life.

* Express your gratitude for what is happening as if it is in existence already.

* Believe that by setting your intentions, they are already done.

Letting go of resistance to doing things that are in your best interest is essential for realizing the desired results of your intentions. If you say you want to be stronger and healthier, but you keep convincing yourself not to get off the couch, you are practicing self-sabotage, then you berate yourself because you are not succeeding when all you had to do is get up off that couch. *What can you do or start right now to align your life with your intention?* Whatever it is, do it *now*!

In the movie *The Secret,* they say, "Thoughts become things." You can harness the power to create the life of your dreams. Let your vision board guide the way.

PRACTICE: JOURNALING YOUR VISION BOARD

Now that you have created your vision board, write about the experience in your journal. Creating your vision board brings your world and priorities into focus. Write about what you are doing to support the desires you illustrate on your board. *What will you do to enable what you indicated on your board to happen, knowing that it is already done in the grand perspective of things?* Also, write a journal entry stating your intentions and affirmations related to your future. By following these steps, you can activate your vision with ease and grace.

KEY TIPS FOR CHAPTER TWELVE

* Discover what is inspiring to you in the future.
* Explore what your 'best life' would look like.
* Create your vision board and look at it daily, activating your vision.

TAKE ACTION

HAPPINESS HABITS

Your Intention

* Write an *Intention* of the overarching intention you will accomplish by creating your vision board.

I intend to _____

_____

_____

_____

_____

Your Gratitude

* Write why you are *grateful* that you completed your vision board.

I am happy and grateful that _____

_____

_____

_____

_____

Your Happiness

* When looking at your vision board, *which three things on the board make you smile the most?*

_____

_____

_____

_____

Your Affirmation

* Write a *positive affirmation* about what you are accomplishing in
your life right now.

I am _____

_____

_____

_____

_____

_____

CHAPTER 13
SERVING OTHERS

"The best way not to feel hopeless is to get up and do something. Don't wait for good things to happen to you. If you go out and make some good things happen, you will fill the world with hope; you will fill yourself with hope.

—BARACK OBAMA

There likely will come a point in your grieving where you say, "Enough. I can't continue what I am doing. There has to be more to life. There has to be something I can do to feel better." And you are right. There is. Chances are, you are wondering what you are supposed to be doing to help ease the sorrow and move on. Nine months after Ron died, I knew I *had* to be doing something, and it turned out that *something* for me was writing a book. I had been searching for help, so I turned to books, and I read many. While most were somewhat helpful, none resonated with me on a deeper level. And, since I am a writer and have been teaching writing for many years, I realized that I could help others by writing my story and including stories of others' experiences with loss. I knew my book had to be about happiness because that is what I wanted to feel despite my loss. While writing my book and setting up my social media platform, I came to know many people who are grieving, and while my support helped them on their paths, their stories helped me know how to help others with the same challenges.

Almost every person I talked to about how they have dealt with their loss has told me the same thing, that there came a point when the best thing they could do for themselves was to find a way to help others. The more ways I found to help others who were grieving, the better I felt. I know this will happen for you when you put your passion and willingness to work in ways that bring joy to those you serve and yourself.

WAYS TO SERVE

I'll start with my creative friend Maryann. She writes her thoughts in her blog *Barefoot Thoughts of an Empath*. Her post, *The Love Fairy,* tells of a beautiful project she created. She starts by saying, "Unless you've been there, truly you can only imagine the difficulties associated with the loss of the love of your life. I have had difficulty since my husband changed his residency to the heavens. I have not been able to shake the overwhelming daily sadness." She had read about a woman who wrote anonymous love letters and left them around New York City. She realized how much she, when working under the pressure of the business world, would love to receive a note of love, so she decided to write some love letters herself. She wrote "about random support and encouragement . . . and unconditional love," hoping to brighten the day of a stranger.

Maryann created colorful, beautiful, hand-decorated, care-filled cards with long notes of love and inspiration. She signed each "The Love Fairy" and left them at random places throughout the community with a big note on the outside of the envelope that said, "This is for You! Yes, you, looking at this envelope." Of course, she never knew the actual reaction people had to reading her messages, but by writing the messages, she started on her journey to finding joy and was grateful for that.

In Maryann's words,

"I'm sharing all of this with the hope that you, too,
will start writing random love letters and leaving
them for people whom you have never met before to find.
People need encouragement.
People need validation.
People need to know they are appreciated.
People need to know they are loved...even if only by a perfect stranger.
Write from your heart.
Perhaps it will make a difference in your life.
For sure, it will make a difference in the life of the
person's life who finds it."

Maryann demonstrates how a random, anonymous act of kindness can lift your spirits and bring joy to a total stranger while also bringing joy to yourself. *So, what can you do?* Think about things you already like to do. *How can you combine what you enjoy with a way to help or bring joy to others?* For instance, I love to take pictures on my phone. Here in Maui, I am always surrounded by and inspired by the endless beauty. I have made note cards using my photos and given them as gifts. My granddaughter Katie suggested that I make some with positive thoughts inside that I could send to her sister-in-law Alexis who was dealing with cancer, so I created several cards to send to her. When she was feeling better, her sister-in-law let me know how they inspired her and that she had actually had some of them framed to hang in her room to remind her of the positive thoughts she felt when she looked at them.

After Bonnie shifted her career path to become a Creative Grief Support Practitioner and a Certified Life-Cycle Celebrant, she said, "Helping is what feels best to me and what truly makes my life feel meaningful . . . As a whole, I make a point to help someone in some way every day."

After the death of his mother, my trainer Ellis was able to incorporate serving others into his career. He had the opportunity to work with a man going through chemotherapy. The man wanted to keep his strength the best he could as his body was dealing with the harsh effects of the medications. Ellis taught safety, form, and technique through each exercise. Helping his client was especially challenging as he discovered that his compassion was the same as when Ellis was dealing with his mother's sickness. That experience helped Ellis find peace, and he's grateful that the man is doing well.

When Sheri attended a workshop I facilitated, she told me her mother died of breast cancer, so she found comfort in fundraising for cancer research. I talked to many survivors of catastrophic illnesses and their families who find peace, comfort, and joy in doing what they can to support the research that hopefully prevents others from going through what they are going through.

One Christmas, my adult son Jason asked if we could bake cookies for the local homeless shelter because his friends stayed there. We spent all day making many different kinds of cookies, then took big platters to the shelter. The people there laughed and hugged and gobbled up the cookies that they said reminded them of better times. I was thrilled to spend time with Jason and enjoyed watching him make his friends happy.

My neighbor Robin called the local women's shelter to ask what she could do to help during the holiday season. They said the women and children there would love a little pampering. Robin started asking her friends and came up with the idea to bring in beauty professionals to do massage, make-up, manicures, and hair. I asked if I could provide food, so Jason and I created gourmet appetizers, cupcakes, and cookies. The women were in tears—most saying they had never had anyone take care of them before. Cooking and baking for others made my holidays much brighter when dealing with my loss.

Tom, a world-renowned ceramic sculptor, has been battling cancer for many years. He's been told to put his affairs in order more than once. Despite hearing those instructions, Tom smiles and keeps a wonderfully positive attitude. He goes camping with his wife every chance they get, provides herbal medications that are especially good for cancer-related pain to anyone who asks, and always creates works of art. His lovely smile and warm hugs always amaze me.

After her father's death, my friend Carla became the main support system for her mother, taking her to appointments and out to lunch, helping her with shopping, and working in her father's garden. Carla feels the importance and appreciates the opportunity to work together with her mother to deal with her father's passing.

EXPANDING YOUR SERVICE

Many people I know find another country they can serve in. My neighbor Jeff goes to Mexico to build houses for those in need. Ingrid went to Africa to volunteer with Heifer International™ to help communities to work together to end world hunger. Clara volunteered in an orphanage in South Africa that cared for infants whose mothers had died of AIDS. Wendy went to New Orleans after Hurricane Katrina to help with health care and housing for the victims. All these people wanted to do more after volunteering for the first time and continue to give back in helpful ways.

My good friend Alda has a very loving, friendly, well-trained dog. She decided to find a place that trains dogs to become service animals and where she could visit people in long-term care facilities with her dog. The people appreciate her dog so much, her dog loves the attention, and Alda feels more love all around.

While riding his bicycle to the store on an errand for his mother, Linda's son was hit and killed by a drunk driver. Though devastated, Linda had to find a way to help her channel her anger and frustration around the preventable tragedy. She became very involved with Mothers Against Drunk Driving™, presenting to people how her life was affected by her son's death in hopes that others would be influenced by her story to not drive after drinking.

When you give some of your time or resources to others, you can obtain rewards in your health and general well-being. In the book, *The Life You Save: How to Do Your Part to End World Poverty*, author Peter Singer says: "A survey of 30,000 American households found that those who gave to charity were 43% more likely to say they were 'very happy' about their lives than those who did not give, and the figure was very similar for those who did volunteer work for charities as compared to those who did not." And, "In a study commissioned by the UnitedHealth Group™, most survey participants reported feeling both physically and mentally healthier after a volunteer experience. Most participants cited mood improvement, lower stress levels, an enriched sense of purpose, and just feeling healthier due to volunteering." "The Corporation for National Community Service revealed that volunteering improves self-esteem, reduces high blood pressure, increases endorphin production, and enhances the immune system." Any time you spend serving others benefits you and those you serve.

MAKE VOLUNTEERING WORK FOR YOU

While volunteering and giving back seems like something good to do, it isn't always easy. When you are inspired to volunteer, think about why you are offering your help. If your loss seems overwhelming and you need to dive into something and spend too much time there, you won't have time left over to deal with your own loss. As with anything, seek a healthy balance. If you volunteer to help those grieving, you may start to feel overwhelmed by the loss of those you are serving, which, in turn, will make your loss seem to worsen. If this happens to you, consider volunteering somewhere different, like an animal shelter, an art program, or an after-school program. Find something where you can experience joy and even love.

When you volunteer, it is natural to want to feel appreciated, but people you serve may not realize the importance of expressing appreciation. Find someplace to volunteer where what you do is rewarding, and if you get thanked, it's an added bonus. For instance, if you are volunteering in an animal center and the people working there are so busy that you don't interact much with them, enjoy your interaction with the animals. Animals tend to love unconditionally, especially those who are helping them.

Another issue that can come up is the natural tendency to assume that the grief of others is like your own, and if you can deal with it, so can they. Though I have had many experiences with grief in addition to the deaths of my husbands, each of the experiences was unique. The deaths occurred at different times in my life, and they all came from different circumstances, from sudden death to accidents, to suicide, to murder, to cancer, to lengthy terminal illnesses. I can't compare one of those deaths to the other or my reactions to the different deaths, and I can't compare my experience to the experience someone else feels. You can listen, be there, and offer your love and support.

When you decide to volunteer, you can find many benefits, such as:

Perspective: Move outside your environment and get a new perspective by helping others in need. Volunteering often fosters gratitude for the life you do have. Through volunteering, you may find yourself feeling gratitude: I am grateful I have a home; I am grateful for food to eat; I am grateful for the people who love me. Let your gratitude guide you to know how to best serve those you are volunteering with.

Intangible Rewards: Knowing that what you do makes a positive difference in someone else's life, even a stranger, is a reward. No prize you win, or money you earn will feel better than a smile or a hug from someone you have served. You will feel a flood of intangible treasures that go beyond monetary compensation.

Purpose: A common feeling is not knowing what to do next. By finding a way or a place to volunteer, you will find a reason to get up, get out of your home, and be with people. The more passionate you are about what you are volunteering to do, the stronger purpose in your life you will experience.

Joy: The biggest reward you can give yourself is *finding joy in what you do*. When you find joy in what you are doing, everything feels better. And the joy you experience makes it all worth the effort.

All these examples of individuals volunteering are designed to give ideas of what you could do. You can start with a small effort. Every service to others counts. You can make new friends who are interested in the kinds of things you are interested in. Whatever you choose to do, the world will be a better place because of your service. And you will discover joy in the process.

PRACTICE: THE POWER OF COMPASSION

Meditate on the power of compassion that comes with serving others. Breathe slowly and deeply, experiencing with each breath the feeling of compassion for yourself and others. When you complete your meditation, explore in your journal all the ways you can think of volunteering or serving someone else. Let your ideas flow freely, and discover your next act of kindness. And after you complete that act, write in your journal again about how it felt and what you will do next to take action on your volunteering ideas.

KEY TIPS FOR CHAPTER THIRTEEN

* Find ways to volunteer in your community or another country.
* Help individuals heart to heart; make it personal to you.
* Know how changing others helps you heal and feel better unconditionally.

TAKE ACTION

HAPPINESS HABITS

Your Intention

* Write an *Intention* about what you are doing or will soon be doing to serve others.

I intend to _____

_____

_____

_____

_____

Your Gratitude

* Write about your *gratitude* for a service someone has done for you to brighten your life, or you can write about services you do for others.

I am happy and grateful that _____

_____

_____

_____

_____

_____

Your Happiness

* Write about a service you would like to do for others and how doing that service would make you feel.

_____

_____

_____

_____

_____

Your Affirmation

* Write a *positive affirmation* about what you must release to be fully open to serving others.

I am _____

_____

_____

_____

_____

_____

_____

_____

CHAPTER 14

REVISIT YOUR JOY

"Live on a natural high."
—MAGIC JOHNSON

Joy can be expressed in so many ways. Everyone has their own definition of joy. You may find joy by spending time with friends, hiking in the woods, reading a good book, singing in a choir, knitting a scarf, watching a play, or going to a concert. Joy is whatever brings you great pleasure or happiness.

Think about how you feel when you find a picture of your loved one or when a special memory comes to mind. While these experiences may bring a few tears, a smile can also come with them. I can honestly say I feel grief and joy simultaneously—and that's both okay and positive.

Ron and I used to talk about joy. He said being happy was merely being content, but that being joyful was way beyond happy, a high level of pure delight and bliss. He felt that feeling joy was an ultimate goal in life. Whenever I think about those conversations, I smile. Living with him was pure joy for me, but initially, living without him was not. What has helped me find my joy again came from contemplating what Ron would have wanted for me. I know Ron always wanted me to smile and smile genuinely. Anything I was doing was worth smiling about, he insisted, whether we were talking to each other or I was typing, reading, cooking, or walking. *Anything worth doing is worth smiling about.* Ron said if I couldn't experience joy in what I was doing, I needed to find something else to do.

Living from the perspective of joy has helped me to change my life. For a long time after Ron's transition, I didn't feel much like smiling until I realized that finding my joy again was the best thing I could do to honor him. He would want happiness for me, so I set out to find a renewed connection with joy.

People may tell you you are stuck in your loss when you keep thinking about your loved one, but that's not true. The bond of love goes on forever, and you will likely feel that love in many different ways. For instance, maybe your loved one had a chair where they liked to sit. I know Ron's chair is on our lanai (back porch), where he would spend hours enjoying the birds, the flowers, the trees, and the blue skies. Other people will sit there now, and I always think of him when they do. And my chair, though it swivels, is usually aimed toward his chair as that was the way it was when we talked or sat together. *Where are memories of your loved one around your home?* Practice looking at things they loved and smile. Feel the joy they felt. The more often you smile that loving smile, the more joy you will feel inside of you.

JOY AND HAPPINESS ARE POSSIBLE

Coming to terms with my losses does not mean that I don't still feel those losses from time to time. For instance, I have my moments when special events happen, like weddings and funerals of loved ones, graduations, birthdays, or celebrations. Tears may come over Jacques or Ron, them not getting to make these new memories with me. I deal with these things by trying to make new events the best they can be. I stay involved with their children. I made the bridal bouquet for my new daughter-in-law Jennifer when she and Jacques's son Stephen married. I did all the flowers when Jacques's granddaughter Isabel married, and Ron even performed at the wedding ceremony. I sent Sydney, another granddaughter of Jacques, his books that had been translated into Chinese when she graduated from high school because she had learned

Chinese. I follow Jacques's granddaughter Katie on social media, who sings and plays upright bass in concerts around the world. I love watching Ron's only grandchild, Jet, growing up, and am so grateful he got to spend some time with him. And I love seeing the success of Ron's daughter Saffronia, his son Yusef, and daughter-in-law Anhthu. Staying in touch with the families keeps the love and joy alive for us all.

Spending time with family, doing extra helpful things, and creating new memories can bring joyful experiences into your life. *What can you do with friends or family that you shared with your loved ones?*

What else can you do now that you know will bring you joy?

Navigating joy and loss together is doable and healthy. Here are a few things to keep in mind in the process:

* **First, take care of you.** When you know an event is coming up that may trigger sad feelings for you, try spending some time exploring how you feel in your journal. Pour everything out onto the page by writing your emotions. Then take some time to meditate. When the event occurs, remember to smile and find something that is happening that brings you joy.

* **Do something physical.** If you start down that sad, weepy path, get up and move. Put on some music and dance in the kitchen. Put cheery music on your headphones and go for a walk. Swim some laps. Ride the bike at the gym. Walk on the beach. Go to the mall and window shop. Get moving, and smile while you move.

* **Celebrate!** Invite a neighbor for a cup of tea or a glass of something you can linger over together. Talk about things that make you happy. Recall the last time you each laughed out loud. Celebrate that it is just a Tuesday or that the dog got a haircut. Make it fun, silly, and unstressful!

* **Honor yourself.** Write an entry in your journal about all the good things you have been doing. *How have you been helping others? What have you been doing to help yourself?* Post something special you did on Facebook, like taking food over to a friend. You may even inspire others to do something similar.

* **Share your love.** The more time you spend aware of the love you give and receive, the better you will feel. Give a big, genuine hug to

a friend. I got a wonderful hug that made my whole week! Send a love note to someone you haven't talked to in a while. Love yourself up with a bubble bath or hot tub dip. Light some candles at the table when you eat dinner. Candles represent love, comfort, and beauty to me. Light them often.

* **Get creative.** Draw or paint a picture. Try a new recipe. Take a class. Write a poem. Take pictures of flowers when you are on your walk. Go to an art store or craft shop and find something that interests you. Anything you make is beautiful simply because you took the time to make it.

Whatever you do, remember to smile and bring joy to what you are doing. Smiling helps trigger endorphins, the happiness hormones which help you feel good physically and reduce stress.

Sometimes when focusing on joy, your monkey mind will keep trying to get you to focus on what makes you sad instead. When your focus shifts to negativity, consciously decide to focus on beauty. We are surrounded by beauty and can find examples everywhere. Jacques loved Baroque music. All he had to do was put on one of Bach's Brandenburg concertos to brighten his day. Ron loved jazz, so he'd crank up a Jazz station on Pandora™, and *all was right with the world.* I've gained an appreciation for Baroque, Jazz, and other music like Michael Franti. So, turn on the music and escape into that beauty.

I love delicious, beautiful food. When I discover that loss affects my appetite, I will take myself somewhere away from home to enjoy something special, like *Ululani's* shaved ice, where I can sit in the sunshine and watch people. Or, I make a special meal and invite a friend over. Friends can really cheer you up. Other times, I opt to go somewhere that is inspiring, like an art gallery, a museum, a forest, or a botanical garden. Your smile will naturally unfold when you are pleased by the beauty surrounding you.

One thing to be aware of when focusing on joy is that many people *seem* depressed. The television bombards us with commercials saying if you want to be better, ask your doctor to prescribe a pill. When they describe all the negative feelings depressed people have, you may say, "What she is saying sounds like me!" But there is a genuine difference between clinical depression and grieving. If you think you are depressed, do talk to your doctor, or you may be able to get help from a counselor or psychologist before taking medications. Be sure to take good care of yourself. Support groups can be really helpful and aid your grieving process. I had the misconception that support groups were sad and teary, but I found a perfect group for me that is fun and uplifting. Our group is a safe place to talk and express our feelings, and we do things together that support each other and bring joy. Find a group that resonates with your personality and happens at a time you can attend and a location that is close to you. Make attending a group easy and effortless so you will be enthusiastic to get up and go on the days you need it most.

Joy comes in all shapes and sizes, in big and small moments. Many times it is unplanned and other times you need to plan and make time for it. The best part about joy is how you feel when you are experiencing joy. You are likely to relax, breathe easier, and feel more comfortable. You may even start craving ways to bring yourself even more joy.

Now is the time to focus on joy. Be open to joy. Look for the joy in all you do. Find places to be and people to be with where you are surrounded by joy. Life is good!

PRACTICE: WHERE'S JOY?

The world became captivated by searching for the character Waldo in pictures of crowds drawn by Martin Handford. In these pictures, it seems that Waldo is all around in his red and white striped shirt. Instead of finding Waldo, let's search for examples of joy, things that make you happy, and things that make you smile. Carry a small journal with you so you can write down every time you discover joy. Then whenever you need a boost, you can simply open your *Joy Journal*, and happy recollections will pour forth. As you write in your journal, include examples of joy that pop into your mind from previous experiences. For example, I remembered when my family was at a casual café, and one of us demonstrated how to get a spoon to stick to her nose. Soon we were all trying it and laughing hysterically. It was so much fun! *When was the last time you laughed?* Write down your joyful experiences so you can enjoy that laughter again!

KEY TIPS FOR CHAPTER FOURTEEN

* Explore the feeling of past joy and remember those precious moments.
* Recognize how past joy relates to the feeling of present joy; find the connection.
* Live consciously in joy, which is a decision you can make.

TAKE ACTION

HAPPINESS HABITS

Your Intention

* Write an *Intention* about how you are moving forward in discovering joy.

I intend to _____

_____

_____

_____

_____

Your Gratitude

* Write three things you are *grateful* for that bring you joy.

I am happy and grateful that _____

_____

_____

_____

_____

Your Happiness

* Write about the last three times you felt genuine *happiness*.

_____

_____

_____

_____

_____

Your Affirmation

* Write three *positive affirmations* that demonstrate joy to you, like "I radiate positivity!"

I am _____

_____

_____

_____

_____

_____

CHAPTER 15

LAUGHTER IS THE BEST MEDICINE

"Live by this credo: have a little laugh and look around you
for happiness instead of sadness. Laughter has always
brought me out of unhappy situations."
−RED SKELTON

When my dear friend Saundy's husband was in and out of the hospital, and people would ask what they could do for her, she asked them to send her funny, clean jokes. I loved that idea and set out to find jokes I could send her. This led me to the odyssey of discovering funny things. I read endless jokes online, and nothing seemed funny because I was trying so hard to find the perfect joke. Then a friend emailed me a joke, and I laughed out loud. I realized it seemed funny because I didn't expect it, so there is something about the element of surprise that helped. I sent Saundy the joke my friend had sent me, and she loved it.

I learned the value of a good laugh in my years directing comedy, especially British farce, for dinner theatre. I worked with my actors to be absolutely serious about the experiences they were acting out. If the actors laughed at themselves, the audience usually didn't laugh. As I watched performances from the audience, I found myself laughing along even though I had heard the lines hundreds of times in rehearsal, and I realized that what made them funny was the freshness of being heard by the audience the first time. And I realized being with all those people laughing, their laughter was contagious—I couldn't help but laugh along.

All that laughter felt so enriching to my spirit. I remember seeing a man I knew in the audience who was terminally ill and was committed to enjoying every moment he had left in his life. When he entered the theatre, he was pale and frail. He sat toward the front of the audience and laughed, enjoying the show so much that the whole audience laughed much more than usual, leading the cast to say that they were the best audience for the show. After the show, my friend had color on his face, and he gave me a warm hug thanking me for the joy we provided. What excellent medicine laughter was for him.

As you focus on reclaiming your joy, smiling and laughter are perfect for exploring. In my research, I found that the concept of laughter being good medicine has been around for a very long time. Medical research shows that smiling and laughing produce these benefits:

* Laughing boosts your immune system.
* Laughter improves the function of blood vessels, increasing blood flow.
* Laughter can help protect from heart attacks.
* Laughter can reduce and relieve pain.
* Laughter allows higher tolerance for discomfort.
* Laughter reduces blood sugar levels.
* Laughter burns calories.
* Laughter eases tension.
* Laughter reduces stress.

All of these are great reasons to use nature's remedy of laughter for so many things!

JOY AND LAUGHTER WORK TOGETHER

My Aunt Mona was a nurse who had trained during World War II and cared for severely wounded soldiers. She married one of her patients who had lost his leg in the war. Their life wasn't easy, but she always handled things with grace and a smile. She was involved in a car accident where her injuries were extreme, and her husband was killed. In her recovery from her injuries after the accident and dealing with her loss, she learned about the movie *Patch Adams*, which is a true story of a physician who, after living with the devastating effects of the war on his family and the ugliness of segregation in the school he attended, decided that instead of wallowing in all that was wrong, would create something better based on love and laughter. He opened a hospital where all treatments were free and based on humor. My aunt watched that movie often and put Patch Adams' philosophy to work. Whenever I visited her, she was in a hospital bed in her living room, always sitting up with a smile and making us laugh. I couldn't help but smile around her. She recovered after the accident and continued to share her joy with the patients in the doctor's office where she worked. She was the perfect example of the value of smile, laughter, and joy in healing.

Whenever Ron caught me with a serious face, he'd remind me to smile. Sometimes he'd flash his big, beautiful smile at me since he knew I couldn't help but smile back. Other times, he would turn my face toward a mirror, which usually made me laugh, seeing how serious I was. Occasionally, I don't feel like smiling, so when I feel like that, I practice the old adage: *Fake it until you make it.* The key is to smile big. When I do a demure little smile with barely turned-up lips, that doesn't help much, but it does remind me to smile with my whole face. A big smile is called a *Duchenne smile*, where you feel all the muscles in your face brighten up. Your laugh lines around your eyes pop up, and it feels really good. Try practicing in front of a mirror. You might even laugh at your poses—laughter is great medicine!

As you focus on reclaiming your joy, smiling and laughter are perfect for exploring. Knowing why we laugh and smile can remind us to practice it more. The purpose of laughing is to bring people together. Start paying attention whenever you hear laughter. *Where are you? Who is laughing? What are they doing?* People rarely laugh alone. If I watch something funny on television, I can enjoy it without laughing, but when I am watching it with someone else, we usually laugh together. When you go to see a comedian, funny movie, or play, chances are people are laughing out loud, and you can tell more about a person's personality by how they laugh. My mother was serious, but sometimes when we would go out to dinner as a family, I would say something that made her laugh. Her laugh was so unexpected that I couldn't help but laugh also, and we'd get the giggles together. At first, our family would look at us like we were crazy or embarrassing them, but then they would join in, and often others in the restaurant started laughing too. That crowd mentality of joy created a positive vibe in the whole room.

Laughing together creates or restores a positive emotional atmosphere vital in any relationship. When we laugh, we trigger the release of pleasure-inducing neurochemicals in our brain, we breathe faster, and our heart rate goes up. Laughing causes more oxygen to surge through our blood, increasing our energy and giving us a kind of natural high. Laughter creates a positive mood which works with our sense of humor to support good health. The neurochemical dopamine is considered the "reward molecule" and helps to make you feel good when you accomplish your goals. You can also trigger dopamine by eating dark chocolate or avocados, drinking green tea, adding turmeric and black pepper to your food, and listening to music. There are so many ways to add some joy to your life. Try one, and when it feels good, try more!

What if you don't feel like smiling? That's understandable. Sometimes after a loss, it is easy to shut down. The voice in your head may be telling you, *What do you have to smile about? You are sad. Don't kid yourself.* When it starts trying to take you down that negative path, be aware of what is happening and make a conscious decision to cheer yourself up.

Yesterday I wasn't feeling my best, I had heard some bad news, and I was letting it affect me. I had to get some groceries, so when I got to the store, I thought I would not reflect my negativity on anyone else; I set out to feel better. I started by holding the door for someone while smiling, and that person smiled back making me feel more like smiling. I started smiling at anyone I made eye contact with, and they smiled back, making me feel like smiling more. When I got to the checkout line, the person behind me only had one item, so I invited her to go before me. She was excited and told the cashier how kind I was. Then the next person who came up behind me only had one item, so I did it again, and she was happy, then the cashier was especially nice to me. I thanked her, thanked the person who bagged my groceries, and left the store feeling much better!

SMILE OFTEN

When I see a young child, I always smile at them. When children are young, they have little to no barriers smiling back at you. They may even giggle, and chances are the adult with them will smile, also. There is nothing like the laugh or giggle of a toddler to get you laughing. They are so wide open with their laughter and love of life. Smiling is definitely contagious—pass it on every chance you get.

Here are a few ideas to try:

* Move toward laughter. When you hear it, see what's funny so that you can laugh also.
* Bring humor into your conversations. Tell a joke or recall a funny experience.
* Laugh at yourself. When you do something silly, be the first to laugh.
* If you start feeling sorry for yourself, recognize what you are doing and find the humor in it.
* Surround yourself with reminders to smile. Keep pictures of your favorite people with big smiles on their faces—smile and say hi to them when you look at them to create a smile in you.
* Watch comedies and comedians. Decide to find things to watch on television that will make you laugh and feel good.
* Read funny books.
* Find positive things to focus on.
* Spend time with fun friends.
* Email jokes or funny things to friends and ask them to send you funny things.
* Tickle a baby and watch the laughter.
* Hang around with people who like to have fun.

Mike Huey and Bob Anderson created The Fabulous Bakersfield Boys, a musical parody act that became hugely popular through their ability to take familiar songs and write personalized lyrics that made people laugh. They poked fun at the politics of the day, the actions of leaders in the community, and their friends. I loved going to their shows because people would laugh so hard they almost couldn't catch their breath, and everybody laughed together. Mike is a doctor and loved sharing humor's healing power, which was often as therapeutic as the medicine he practiced. When humor is personalized, it usually increases the laughter.

Silent film star Mary Pickford was used to taking much responsibility for the films she was in. As she became popular, she started to work for a big film company where she and her friend, writer Frances Marion, decided to create the film *Poor Little Rich Girl*™. After her father died in an accident, Pickford had been supporting her family as a child actress and never had a chance to be a child herself. Making *Poor Little Rich Girl*, she got to play the part of a young girl and learned what it was like to play. They had so much fun making the movie that they knew it would be a big hit. When they went to a private preview screening with the producers, Pickford and Marion dressed in business attire and entered a room filled only with men. Because music for the silent movies was always performed live, they didn't hire musicians for the screening, so they watched the silent movie in a dark silent room with a bunch of dour men who didn't even smile. The men proclaimed that the movie was a disaster, that no one would like it, and that they would all lose their money and reputations. The movie was released because it was under contract with many theaters already. The men were shocked and the ladies were vindicated that combining the film with music and an appreciative audience was a wild success. Laughter and joy come from combining the right elements, whether it is who you are with or what is happening. Laughter can erupt at any moment; when it does, enjoy!

The most important thing you can do for yourself to reclaim your joy is to commit to your own happiness. Put yourself in a place where others are laughing. Spend more time in positive situations. Smile often and laugh every chance you get.

PRACTICE: LAUGH QUEST

Find at least ten jokes or funny stories and write them out in your journal. Practice sharing these funny things, one at a time. You can tell them in person or send them a text or email. You could write it on a note to send to a friend. Make it your quest to get at least ten different laughs. If someone responds with something funny, add that to your list in your journal. Challenge your friends to find appropriate jokes and funny stories. When you hear that a friend is facing a challenge or is feeling a little blue, or tell them a joke. You'll both feel better!

KEY TIPS FOR CHAPTER FIFTEEN

* Feel how endorphins help heal the body when you laugh.
* Discover where to find funny things that will make you laugh.
* Find how to regularly laugh and the benefits that laughing will bring.

TAKE ACTION

HAPPINESS HABITS

Your Intention

* Write an *Intention* about who or how many people you will get to smile or laugh with this week.

I intend to _____

_____

_____

_____

_____

Your Gratitude

   * Write three things that have made you smile or laugh during the week that you are *grateful* for.

I am happy and grateful that _____

_____

_____

_____

_____

Your Happiness

   * Make a list of at least ten jokes, funny stories, comedies, or comedians that really strike your funny bone, and share things on your list to encourage people to smile. And keep adding more things to your list as you think of them.

_____

_____

_____

_____

Your Affirmation

   * Write a *positive affirmation* that starts with the words "I am happiest when . . . ."

I am happiest when _____

_____

_____

_____

_____

_____

PERSONAL NOTES

CHAPTER 16

SHOW APPRECIATION

"As we express our gratitude, we must never forget that the highest appreciation is not to utter words, but to live by them."
–JOHN F. KENNEDY

Throughout this book, we have explored the importance of gratitude. In this chapter, we will go a step further into the gratitude process so that you can find both the benefits of giving and receiving. Let's say someone helped you with a big project you were working on, and their help made a difference in the project's success. The first step in showing gratitude would be to write exactly what you were grateful for and what that person did to help you. Next would be showing that appreciation. *How can you express your gratitude differently than you usually do?* The answer is to be creative.

Being creative with your gratitude will help you feel the benefits of expressing your thanks in addition to the experience of witnessing the effects of your gratitude on the person you are thanking. Finding ways to be creative in this process can be fun and help you to foster great relationships.

I recently coordinated a silent auction fundraiser for an organization I admire. A friend asked me to help her, and I said yes. Doing all that was involved in creating a silent auction took a lot of time and creativity because I was starting from scratch. Still, I enjoyed the process and was able to acquire many more donations than they had in the past, and that led to a big boost in the funds raised. I was happy with what I accomplished, which was very rewarding for me. I was surprised by the appreciation shown to me by several people who expressed their gratitude by giving me praise and hugs. They even presented me with a beautiful plumeria lei, a traditional way to say *"mahalo,"* thank you in Hawaiian. I have worked on many projects for organizations before, and I have never been shown so much appreciation. I am sure part of that comes from Hawaiian culture, but it was so much more; it made me want to continue to be around these loving, appreciative people and do more to support their cause.

Having my work noticed by others demonstrated to me the importance of appreciation. Since then, I have started emphasizing appreciation in my everyday activities and adding in special acts of kindness. I now start each day by writing in my gratitude journal, and as I write, I consider how I can show my appreciation for all I am grateful for. I do this in the simplest of ways; by making eye contact with those who I am speaking to and truly paying attention to what is being said. I listen instead of trying to figure out what I will say next. I learn so much more by paying attention, and I have no problem saying what I want when I know they are finished speaking. This is one of the many ways I have increased my commitment to showing as much appreciation as possible and mirroring what I believe is essential kindness.

APPRECIATION GOES A LONG WAY

When you reach a point in your grieving process where you deeply appreciate all that unfolds, you will want to show it more and express it often. To support you in making appreciation a part of your constant practice, I've made a long list of ways to show appreciation, with many ideas and examples of how to incorporate gratitude and kindness into your everyday life. I find the more I focus on others, the less I worry about myself, and the more joy I get to experience.

Try some of these ideas, and then have fun creating additional ways to express how you feel when you are in appreciation of others.

* **Find something to appreciate in everything you encounter.** Maybe the sky is especially blue, or someone had a great smile when they spoke to you. What you appreciate does not have to be material or tangible. It can be as simple as a feeling.

* **Look for the good in every situation.** We get conditioned to seek out what is wrong or needs to be corrected. Recognize when you do that and turn your thoughts around. For instance, if you find yourself upset with someone who is late to an event you are hosting, instead, be grateful that they arrived safely.

* **Help whenever you can.** My friend Sharon volunteers to do the dishes after a potluck that we attend regularly. She has the opportunity to meet others who are helping out, and they make cleaning up fun by doing it together.

* **Be there for someone.** Think of a friend who could use support. Often people just need someone to listen. They don't necessarily want advice, they just want to be heard by someone who won't judge.

* **Share your delight around receiving.** When you display a thoughtful gift a friend has given you, that friend can feel the gift of your appreciation.

* **Help someone.** Help a friend to move, clean out the garage, take unwanted items to the dump, or fix a healthy dinner. Helping others can be a boost to your sense of well-being when you selflessly serve someone you care about.

* **Stay calm in a time of stress.** Recently we had a hurricane warning on Maui, and at the time people were rushing to the grocery stores to buy out all the food and water. In watching the panic around me, I decided to stay calm because being worried and upset wouldn't serve me. In my calmness, I was able to bring peace around me. And, we all are more prepared for next time.

* **Say you are sorry.** When there is a reason to be sorry for something, express that sorrow. When we don't apologize, we tend to hold on to whatever the problem was, and it gets harder to let go which turns it into a burden. Releasing guilt over something is so freeing.

* **Give big hugs and warm handshakes.** A woman I didn't know came to me to talk about her loss. A friend had suggested that I could help her. We talked for a couple of hours, and when we were done, she gave me the biggest, warmest hug with tears in her eyes. I haven't seen her again, but I will always remember her gratitude.

* **Give away something of yours that you think someone would enjoy.** Before you donate or discard something, consider which of your friends might love to have what you no longer need. I've known many people who have gifted gently used clothes that their children had quickly outgrown or equipment they no longer needed.

* **Give big tips.** You'd be surprised how many people don't tip at all, and since there is the assumption that people will tip, traditionally service staff get a very low hourly wage. Giving a big tip, especially when your service is good, is deeply appreciated, and should also make you feel good.

* **Respect the time of others.** When any kind of gathering is scheduled for a certain time, having everyone there on time shows respect for all who come. Timeliness takes the pressure off the leader of the gathering and allows time for whatever needs to be accomplished. Being on time also goes for when you plan to meet someone. Having to wait, wondering if someone will show up, is no fun.

* **Share the joy of others.** When someone you know has a happy event, be sure to recognize it. Facebook is a good place to congratulate someone, as is calling someone or sending a note or email. Celebrate anything like a birthday, anniversary, or award, or other things like a new hairstyle, a new grandchild, or a great new recipe. Find fun things to celebrate.

* **Introduce people who may be good for each other.** Try introducing people you think will have things in common. Or, recommend friends for services, like when you know someone great at doing taxes or someone great at car detailing. When you see a place for rent close by, suggest it to a friend who could become your neighbor.

* **Donate to charity.** Many non-profit organizations cannot survive without the support of individuals. Find opportunities to support something you feel strongly about. What organizations or people do you like to support? Your support could be a financial donation,

but it could also be goods or services you could provide. Nonprofit organizations are always looking for people to serve on their boards.

* **Volunteer.** There are endless ways to serve others. Can you take dogs for a walk from the local SPCA? Could you make sandwiches every week to deliver to the homeless, where you know homeless people gather? Maybe you could volunteer to rock babies at the hospital when parents can't be there all the time. Find something that interests you and do it.

* **Share what you can.** Every week people come together for what we call *produce share*. All of us have gardens and fruit trees and have more food than we can use individually, so we share it with whoever comes. We've also become friends in the process. And in our neighborhood, we are always sharing food when a recipe is too big for one family, or we will make cookies or cake to share sometimes to spread some joy.

* **Use your talents.** *Kapuna* (wise elders in Hawaii) share oral history with island children to keep their culture alive. We all have talents. Discover a way you can use your talent to help someone else.

* **Personalize the things you give.** When Ron and I moved into our first home, Rose, a friend on the island, noticed that the small window in the front door was cracked, so she created a beautiful stained-glass window for us to install. Something especially made as a gift or chosen with the interests of the receiver in mind is always appreciated.

* **Visit people**. Often the sick, elderly, or grieving spend much time alone. Their days can be brightened by the gift of time. I know that especially when my feelings were heavy, I so appreciated when someone would drop by or call. You don't have to spend a long time with them. Sharon participated with a foundation called, *By Your Side*, where she volunteered to sit with terminally ill people who didn't have friends and family to visit them. I've often thought what a wonderful gift that was for her to give to strangers.

* **Smile when you ask for assistance.** So often, we are in a hurry when we need help from someone and don't really pay attention to how we ask. When you smile at your server when you ask for more coffee or smile at the office worker when you ask to make an appointment, you might make their day. Try making eye contact and smiling each time you ask for help.

* **Be gracious when complimented.** We are taught to be humble, so we are often uncomfortable and don't know how to react when someone compliments us. When you show respect to the person offering a compliment, you are essentially complimenting them back. And it's always okay to take credit for a job well done.
* **Thank people for encouraging you.** I often express appreciation for people who have been encouraging me in the process of writing my book. The encouragement from others is priceless and recognizing the people who give it is essential.
* **Share positivity.** My friend Shirley Brewer sends me a funny or beautiful text every day which reminds me of her laughter and makes me smile.

There are endless ways to express your appreciation to others. This list is just a few ideas to get you thinking about things you can do to increase your levels of appreciation for those around you. And as you get started, offer appreciation to yourself first. Recognize that you are striving to live your best life by taking good care of yourself. Think of something you did lately where you really impressed yourself and give yourself lots of appreciation for the effort and results you made.

Last week I went to an appointment at the wrong time—I had written the incorrect time on my calendar. In the past, I would have been upset and tried to talk the person into working me into the schedule to accommodate my mistake. Instead, I smiled and said I'd see her when I came back later that day at the right time. I took myself to a coffee shop I had wanted to visit, treated myself to a yummy Golden Milk, which I hadn't tried before, and people-watched while I waited. It was good to relax, and I realized there was no reason to stress myself out over these minute mistakes. Instead, it was far more enjoyable to be appreciative of the time I was able to spend doing something new.

Appreciate each moment you spend doing whatever you do. Show appreciation to others and to yourself, and take really good care of you.

"Let us be grateful to people who make us happy;
they are the charming gardeners who make our souls blossom."
– Marcel Proust

PRACTICE: SHOWING APPRECIATION

Start by making a list in your journal of good things you have done or do for others. Then, write a thank you letter to yourself for all the special things you do. After, write a journal entry exploring ways you can volunteer or contribute more to people or causes you are passionate about. Start by listing what those causes are, then think of ways you can support them. Decide which projects you would most want to spend your time on. The project doesn't have to be big, only something you would enjoy while helping someone else. Then make a plan and get started!

KEY TIPS FOR CHAPTER SIXTEEN

* Explore things appreciation can be shown for.
* Explore creative ways of expressing appreciation.
* Establishing a practice of showing appreciation as often as possible to as many people as you can.

TAKE ACTION

HAPPINESS HABITS

Your Intention

* *What is your Intention about what you will do today to show someone appreciation?*

I intend to _____

_____

_____

_____

Your Gratitude

* Write what you have done that you are *grateful* that you did, then thank yourself for doing it.

I am happy and grateful that _____

_____

_____

_____

_____

Your Happiness

* *What is something you can do to show appreciation for something special?* Do whatever that is.

_____

_____

_____

_____

Your Affirmation

* *Write what you will do to freely and fully express your appreciation.*

I am _____

_____

_____

_____

_____

_____

_____

_____

CHAPTER 17

DANCING

"If you hit a wall, climb over it, crawl under it, or dance on top of it."
—UNKNOWN

Though I don't consider myself a dancer, I love to dance. As a child, I dreamed of dancing with a tall, handsome man, me in a ball gown and him in a tuxedo guiding me in a beautiful waltz around a dance floor where everyone backed out of our way to watch the beauty of our dancing. While that never happened, some of my sweetest memories with my two husbands involve dancing. Jacques and I frequently went to a nearby hotel that had a great cover band—we would dance and spend time together. Sometimes friends went along, but usually we took this time for ourselves. We relished those special moments.

Two weeks after I met Ron, I had a high school reunion and convinced him to go with me. We hadn't danced together, so I had no idea what to expect. They played a fast, soulful song, and he asked me to dance. He was an amazing dancer, and like in my dream, we cleared the floor, and everyone clapped for us and came up to talk to us when the dance was over. We were the highlight of the reunion, and I realized at that moment that I was in love.

We talked a lot about dancing after that evening, and it turned out he had learned to dance to become popular with the girls. He must have been very popular! I told him how I thought the ideal husband would sweep me into his arms whenever a romantic song came on to dance up close with me even in the kitchen. About a year later, I had to have a complicated surgery on my knee. Ron came to take me to the hospital while it was still dark in the morning, and when I walked into the kitchen, he had one of our favorite songs playing and we danced a long, slow dance. I was so touched that he remembered what I had said and wanted to be sure to dance with me since we didn't know how long it would be before we could dance again.

When Ron and I moved to Maui, I discovered a soul music dance exercise class nearby, so I started attending and meeting local people. Then, Ron's health declined, and I stopped going to classes. A few weeks later, he was feeling good and encouraged me to go to class. When I arrived, everyone said they missed me, and I told them that Ron had been in the hospital and that I needed to be with him. The next week when I arrived, they presented me with a huge basket filled with treats, everything from soups to cookies. They said it was for my husband to help him get better. I was so touched and realized how coming together through dance brought us joy and helped us build community.

I didn't dance for a long time after Ron died. I love to go watch my friends play in a band and sing, and eventually, I was able to get up to dance, all the time knowing that Ron loved to watch me dance and would be happy to see me dancing. Knowing how good I feel when I dance made me think that dancing would be a perfect way to help me reclaim my joy, so I started researching how others deal with loss and dancing.

DANCING CAN HELP WITH GRIEF

Dancer and writer Suzanne Guillette followed the wisdom of Martha Graham, who said, "The body says what words cannot." Guillette added to that by saying, "I needed to use my body to dance through grief. I had thought plenty about grief and loss, but thinking is not feeling. And, when we cut ourselves off from our feelings, the pain gets trapped in the body, causing suffering and disconnection. The body must then also be the instrument for release." She also said, "Instead of working from choreography, I focused on the feelings that came up and let myself *be* danced." Being "danced" makes so much sense to me. With my background as an actress, I remembered feeling totally transformed by the expression I experienced when performing. Dancing is acting without words so that only your movements, in relation to the music, convey your innermost feelings.

Sadness can flow from the dancers' fingertips, while loss can escape from an opening heart. While dancing is a personal expression, the movement is conveyed to the audience through the waves of emotion that travel through the air to reach the personal space of the observer. The feelings that permeate the room and penetrate the psyche of both the dancer and those watching create a unique experience that can lead to healing or, at least, to a contemplation of what happened.

I loved the television series, *So You Think You Can Dance*, which was a competition show trying to find America's favorite dancer. On it, I watched heart-wrenching choreography performed by a dancer who had cancer. I sobbed as I watched the judge's comment, and they also cried. The performance was powerful beyond words. I encourage you to watch it so you can experience the visceral nature of dancing and watching dance.[4]

You don't have to dance yourself to experience the gift of dancing. Watch what you can on YouTube or do a Google search and see how others dance their way through trauma, devastating illnesses, accidents, and reactions to all these things. When dealing with these deep emotions, sometimes speaking about them isn't enough to deal with the feelings and thoughts you are experiencing. Dancing can take you beyond the realm of the usual communication we do through speaking.

DISCOVER YOURSELF IN DANCING

Dancer Stephanie Larson says, "Know this. Dance can heal grief and loss. Spoken language is inadequate to express and process the thoughts,

---

[4] https://youtu.be/PXZwN3CEgXc

moods, sensations, and emotions accompanying bereavement. Dancing enables us to be in the present moment, feeling a sense of groundedness from connecting to our bodies, the earth, and those dancing with us. Through dance, we can value and experience all of our emotions in their authenticity. Pain can arise, be felt, and with a physical gesture, be stomped into the ground or released into the air. Grief can move through like a wave. Instead of lodging deep within us, it can ebb and flow out through the swaying of our shoulders or circling of our hips. Thoughts can come and go while the physicality of the dance reminds us we are alive and that through us our loved ones live on."

You don't have to be a trained dancer to dance. While you can go to a dance class or to your favorite place to dance, you can also dance at home all by yourself. Put on music that expresses how you are feeling and dance along. There is no right or wrong way to dance. Think of it as an expression of your feelings. Use dance to let everything out. Your dance may be slow, sorrowful, or passionate, or it may include stomping, shouting, stretching, spinning, or whatever movement you are inspired to do.

People tend to be sedentary while grieving, but the more you move, the faster you will be able to move forward even if you start by taking a walk in your neighborhood, or stretching in bed before you get up in the morning. Allow your body to get in touch with itself. Pull your knees up to your chest and rock back and forth. Any movement is a beginning.

When you are ready, you can try anything from dance therapy from a qualified professional to dance lessons at a local studio. Consider going to a place that has a good band and you don't have to have a partner, you can dance amongst the crowd. I have friends who play great dance music and sing, and I love to go watch them. Occasionally I'll get up on the dance floor by myself, and there are always others dancing alone which makes it fun. I have had friends ask me to dance, and sometimes I will feel like it, and other times I can't, and either way is okay. Doing what you are comfortable with is what counts.

There are so many types of dancing to try. There is a resurgence of tap dancing, and I know several adults who take lessons. You can find places to line dance or square dance. You could try a ballet class for adult beginners.

I like to go to Zumba classes for exercise. If the first thing you try doesn't work for you, try another. And, remember to crank up the tunes when you are home so that you can get your groove on while you fix dinner. I go to the *Soul Sisters* retreat with Rickie Byars and Greta Sesheta every summer and we do African dance, and we also always have a slumber party with a Soul Train.

I used to love it on *Grey's Anatomy*™ when Meredith and Christina would "dance it out" when they were up against a challenge. If you start to get blue or feel low on energy, put on some tunes and dance it out!

Practice: Move!

Dancing is a fabulous way to get moving, and I highly advise it, though I do realize that not everyone can or wants to dance. Balance is vital for any type of movement; as we age, we often lose some of our natural ability to keep balanced. If movement of any kind is challenging for you, start by doing exercises that can help strengthen your balance. Search YouTube or ask a trainer for help. Then, find a place to do some form of dance. Choose whatever appeals to you the most. If dancing won't work for you, choose another form of movement and incorporate it into your daily practice.

Key Tips for Chapter Seventeen

* The importance of physical expression.
* Other forms of physical expression beyond dancing.
* Establishing a practice of physical expression.

Take Action

HAPPINESS HABITS

Your Intention

* Write what your new *Intention* is to bring more movement into your life, then do it!

I intend to _____

_____

_____

_____

_____

Your Gratitude

* Write what movement you are *grateful* to be able to do. Include how movement makes you feel. If you haven't been moving, try dancing or moving in some way before you write your gratitude here.

I am happy and grateful that _____

_____

_____

_____

_____

Your Happiness

* *What about dancing makes you happy? What are your favorite dances to do?*

_____

_____

_____

_____

_____

Your Affirmation

* Write a *positive affirmation* about the movement you commit to doing now every day.

I am

_____

_____

_____

_____

_____

_____

CHAPTER 18

CHANGE

"The only thing that is constant is change."
−HERACLITUS OF EPHESUS

When someone you love passes away, often you long for things to be the way they used to be. Coming to terms with the fact that it will never be as it was can be one of the hardest challenges you have to face when forced to accept change. When you examine life, you can see that nothing stays the same indefinitely. With both Jacques and Ron, though neither complained, they suffered a great deal with their illnesses. When they passed I felt as though I had nothing to go back to; too much had changed. Over time, I realized that I am responsible for my own life and joy, as are you. I had to accept the changes in my life as you too will need to do. Ask yourself, *What change needs to happen for me to lead my best life? What changes can I embrace and learn to appreciate? How is this change supporting my highest good?*

Let's look at some of the changes that have happened in your life and see how you can make positive changes.

  * **Patterns.** You probably had a few patterns in your life that have been the same for a long time, but either there is no longer a need for that pattern, or things are different now. My patterns for the last few years revolved around Ron, cooking for him, spending time with him, and caring for medical matters. Almost everything revolved around time spent together. You may have had patterns like going

to work, spending time with friends, or participating in activities. For instance, Ron played golf for as long as he was able. While he was on the course, I always tried to do something for myself, like get a pedicure or go for a walk on the beach. When I realized I had stopped this self-care habit, I scheduled a pedicure and got back on track with my self-care.

* **Responsibilities.** If your loved one was ill for a while, you had a whole set of responsibilities around that. If your loved one died suddenly or after a short illness, you have a whole *new* set of responsibilities. The key is to identify all your new or continuing responsibilities so you can continue doing them. For instance, bills need to be paid on time, home and maintenance must be kept up, and you may be responsible for going to work every day. Once you identify your responsibilities, make a list and create a plan moving forward. The process of getting organized will relieve the pressure of worrying about what you need to get done. Remember that even though you may have new or different responsibilities—your biggest responsibility is to take care of yourself.

* **Health.** After the death of a loved one, health challenges may emerge. Pay attention to how you are feeling physically. Getting a check-up with your doctor is a good idea to help you recognize any concerns and help you know how to best physically take care of yourself if needed.

* **Priorities.** Initially, your priority is likely to be getting through the day, but as time goes on, you'll discover that everything seems different and that you may have new or different priorities. Maybe you choose to spend more time with loved ones and family that you didn't have time for in the past. Or your priority may now be to financially support yourself or your family and you either need to return to work or find a job. Whatever your priorities are, take special care of yourself and your relationships.

* **Interests.** Often our interests are intertwined with our relationships. You may have spent your time together with activities you both enjoyed that aren't activities you can or would want to do by yourself. Now is the time to discover activities you can do for you

to enjoy. I have discovered a variety of classes at our local art center
and I love what I am learning there. The classes are new to me, and
I am meeting new people. Spend some time considering what you
have always wanted to do, and do that. Everything doesn't have to be
new. Maybe getting together with old friends for dinner or renewing
a hobby you used to love, or rereading books and journals you once
wrote. Pay attention to what interests you, then do those things so
that you can enjoy your interests.

* **Self.** Reflecting back, I see that many changes unfolded after Jacques
  and Ron each died, though they were different. I've always lived
  a busy life with much to do, yet time seemed to stand still when I
  found myself alone. When I realized that time was moving on, even
  when I felt like I wasn't, I realized it was time for me to figure out
  what to do with myself. Take the time for self-reflection, self-care,
  and self-love, and always be self-supportive.

After Ron transitioned, I discovered that I had to decide what to do. For
the first few months, I felt like I was floating with no real purpose in life. That
wasn't a pleasant or comfortable feeling to have. I realized that what I was going
to do for the rest of my life was up to me, so I started actively looking at my
life and paying attention to my wants, needs, and desires. First, I started by
cleaning the house. Not only was I systematically going through everything I
owned, but I also started releasing anything that no longer served me. Here's
a list of things to consider when you are ready to embrace change:

* **Stuff:** When I heard my community association was having a big
  rummage sale, I used that as motivation to get rid of anything I no
  longer used, wore, looked at, needed, or wanted. I was amazed at
  how much stuff I gave away. Giving it all to a good cause helped, and
  I found I was so much lighter when I finished. Now I go through
  my things on a regular basis and am amazed at how much I can give
  away.

* **Organizations:** While participating in organizations you believe
  in and enjoy can fill a special place in your life, when the joy is no
  longer there or the organization itself no longer suits you, letting it
  go can create space for something new, different, or perfect for your

new life. We moved to Maui two years before Ron died. I realized that I was holding on to memberships I wouldn't have any use for from Hawaii, so I let them go. I was hanging on out of habit. Now I am discovering interesting organizations on the island, where I am learning new things and meeting new people. If you don't have any organizations to let go of, you can discover some new ones that would be perfect for you.

* **People:** There will be people in your life who you will no longer feel comfortable with. While I loved and needed to be around people, there were some people that had become toxic to me. They either drained me of energy or were no longer aligned with my priorities. By letting them go with love, I felt a release of tension that I appreciated and gained space for new relationships with people I had more in common with.

* **Activities:** If you are involved in any activities that you no longer enjoy or that are difficult for you to do for any reason, consider not doing them anymore. Jacques and I used to go out dancing or out for drinks with our theatre friends, and when Jacques wasn't with me, I couldn't go anymore. I felt out of place and felt that people weren't comfortable around me. You don't need to participate in anything that makes you uncomfortable, and stopping being involved in those activities will provide more space to find ones you can enjoy now.

* **Habits:** Releasing habits can be the hardest thing to do. We get so used to doing things that no longer serve us that we don't even realize we are doing them. These habits could be something like eating when we aren't hungry, or mindlessly having the television on when we aren't watching anything. Or they could be spending hours on Facebook or playing games on your phone or computer. Look at anything you do that doesn't bring joy into your life, make you stronger, or make you feel happier. You can free up so much time by eliminating these time thieves.

After identifying what you want to release to 'clean house,' plan to actively let it go, maybe not all at once but over time. As you work through this process, you will discover that the more you release, the easier it becomes and the lighter you will feel in the process. Change is good and it is by embracing change that new things are able to emerge.

EMBRACING CHANGE IN OTHER AREAS

As you are embracing chance, you may want to ask yourself what other changes you can implement. For example: *Do you need to change the way you are handling your finances?* Especially if your loved one always did the finances, you may have some learning to do. Or you may discover that you need to have some help around the house, with yard work, or household chores. My finances have become so complicated that I now have a bookkeeper, and I am grateful to have that task off my shoulders. Instead of feeling lost without my loved one, I looked at the change as a way to grow within.

Have you taken care of all the changes in your legal matters? Be sure to change beneficiaries on insurance policies wherever that is needed. You may also need to change who your designated decision maker is on your Durable Power of Attorney, and you may need to make some changes in your will. Be sure to consult an attorney so that everything is in order for you. If you don't have a power of attorney or will, now is the time to take care of that.

If you need to change your current employment or go back to work, carefully decide when is best according to how you are doing. I have heard so many stories about employers not understanding loss and expecting employees to jump right back in as if nothing happened. Maybe now is the perfect time to try a new job or welcome change if you're feeling the need for something new. Whatever you decide about work, be sure it is a decision that you can be happy with even if it means a big change from what you are used to.

People have probably told you not to make big decisions the first year. I always thought whoever said that hasn't had to face the big decisions that happen in the first year of grieving. After Jacques died, I sold our home and bought a new, much smaller one within the first six months. I have never regretted that decision which allowed me to be in a place to begin anew.

Moving may give you the change you need. And in a new place, you may not have daily reminders of difficult experiences. Think carefully about any big decisions, and get support from those you trust who know that new changes will be good for you.

You may experience physical changes in your body which are usually perfectly normal. These changes may be overwhelming or require medical care, but many will pass with time spent taking care of yourself. The usual symptoms are fatigue, headaches, feeling that you are in a fog, losing focus, eating too little or eating too much, getting sick, feeling disconnected, or being afraid. When these symptoms occur, be patient with yourself. Know that your body is adjusting to the changes in your life and will require dedicated self-care.

When discussing change, we are not discussing changing how you feel about your loved one. Find positive ways to honor your memories. I honor Ron and Jacques with my writing and my work helping others through finding their paths back to joy. You may choose to do something like a cancer walk to raise funds for research or volunteer at a dialysis center. My friend Brooke started a nonprofit organization after her daughter died of cancer, leaving an infant behind. She wanted to provide counseling for children who have lost someone dear. Rev. Rachel created a shrine in her home which includes pictures and items that inspire memories of her loved ones. You may choose to do something in honor of your loved one, like making a contribution to a favorite organization or traveling to someplace you always thought you would go to together. Find something special that will make you smile when you think of it, and do it. These kinds of changes have a positive impact and can often help make the adjustment period a little easier.

Change can be challenging, so when you are dealing with it, be sure to take ample care of yourself. Be gentle with yourself as well as gentle with others who don't understand what you are experiencing. And be sure to find joy in the changes that you make and the changes you experience.

"Never say you will try. Say you will."
Rev. Johnnie Coleman

Practice: Affirm Your Changes

In noticing changes you have made or are making, be sure *you are going in the direction you desire.* Writing positive affirmations will help you commit to your new life. Think about a negative thought you have had about yourself in the past, change it to a positive, and make it a supportive affirmation. For example, if you thought, "I can't figure out what to do." Change that to, "I am creative and confident in my next step forward." Or, be even more specific than that. "I am an excellent writer and am creating wonderful poetry." Always start your affirmations with the words "I am," so that you are speaking in the present tense and affirming what *is* happening. Be sure that your affirmations aren't too long so you can easily remember and repeat them. Write three affirmations now, then add more as you move forward to reflect your direction.

Key Tips for Chapter Eighteen

* The meaning of change and the good that comes from it.
* Explore ways you can make changes in your life.
* Discover ways to make personal changes with positive results.

Take Action

HAPPINESS HABITS

Your Intention

* Write an *Intention* about what change you will make, then make a commitment to make that change.

I intend to _____

_____

_____

Your Gratitude

* Write what you are *grateful* for about three things that have changed for you after your loved one died.

I am happy and grateful that _____

_____

_____

_____

_____

Your Happiness

* You can be *happy* now. *What are you happy about that is new to you now?*

_____

_____

_____

_____

Your Affirmation

* Write a *positive affirmation* about what you are changing in your life relating to your grief.

I am _____

_____

_____

_____

_____

_____

_____

_____

CHAPTER 19

THE MUSIC OF LIFE

"Music is the best consolation for a grieving person."
–MARTIN LUTHER KING

Our brains have a pleasure center filled with neurotransmitters that can make us feel exceptionally well with certain stimuli. Music can be a powerful stimulus that triggers these positive receptors. Think of how you feel when you listen to music. *Does different music trigger different emotions in you? Do you associate certain music with certain people, an era of your life, or an experience?* For me, Ron was jazz and Jacques was baroque. If I hear any music from either of those genres, I am immediately transported. Certain songs bring memories that allow me to feel positive sensations. Jacques loved to play his ukulele and sing *Over the Rainbow*, and now that I live in Hawaii, I hear that song all the time, and it's accompanied by a ukulele. I also remember vividly one afternoon early in my relationship with Ron when The Spinner's Song, *Could it Be I'm Falling in Love* came on, and he held my hand and sang along with the song gazing into my eyes as he smiled. These songs create smiles and tears every time I hear them.

Music has been a healing part of my process and I'd like to suggest you use music to support your healing also. You may be asking, *what does music have to do with grief?* Music can unlock emotions and help transport feelings in new and different ways. When we find the music that stimulates those good feelings, we can activate them by putting on the song. Think about times in your life when you have been positively affected by music. For instance, what would Christmas be without Christmas carols? I'll bet you know all the words to many of them. They can remind you of times singing carols by the fire, or the piano, or caroling for your neighbors, or at the Christmas celebration at church. During our first Christmas season in Maui, we were thinking it might be Ron's last Christmas because of his recent critical hospitalizations. We didn't know many people on the island, yet one evening we heard carols coming from outside and discovered that our new friends Ron M, Julie, Shea, Kevin, and Shena had come to share the spirit of the season with us. I cherish the sweet memory of that music that brought me to tears.

Think about when a major tragedy or natural disaster occurs and a song eases us through the event with an impactful song and where people are drawn together for major concerts to fundraise for the victims. These huge events inspire both tears and joy: tears for the tragedy and joy for the help being provided. An early example of collaboration was when Dionne Warwick, Elton John, Gladys Knight, Stevie Wonder, and many other stars sang *That's What Friends Are For* to raise millions for various AIDS organizations. Since then, when there is a large-scale tragic event, musical stars gather to bring support, and iconic songs are created to heal hurting hearts. Music has traditionally been a way to bring people together to sing, to perform, and to listen. These musical events also provide a venue for people to grieve together for their mutual losses.

There may be days in your life when the sadness can be overwhelming, and crawling into bed with sad songs like Mariah Carey and Boyz II Men's, *One Sweet Day,* or Josh Groban's, *To Where You Are,* can help you release the tears and move through the emotions. These songs, which seem sad, actually can be positive and can help you remember or create new memories about your loved one. Or, if you are dragging and you want to feel better, you could put on *Happy* by Pharrell Williams or *Don't Worry, Be Happy* by Bobby McFerrin and sing along, and maybe dance a little. There is research out there that demonstrates how improving our mood can improve our lives and music can help us along the way.

MUSIC FOSTERS HEALING

Music can also help us relieve pain, reduce stress, and ease tension. Background music is used during meditation and to calm people in waiting rooms. Music is often played while you are waiting on hold on your phone. We sing lullabies to babies to rock them to sleep. You also may hear music in elevators to calm the passengers. When boarding a flight, relaxing music is played to relieve the anxiety of those who fear flying. Think about all the music you hear in the background as you go about your daily activities.

In the aftermath of 9/11, Samuel Barber's *Adagio for Strings Opus 11* became the anthem of grief; it was written in 1938 and was not well received, but when it was played after 9/11, people universally related to it. The passionate, powerful, mournful music allowed the listeners to interpret their own memories of the event personally while uniting with others as they listened to the same music. Usually, though, we aren't in a situation where there are millions to share our loss, but we can still use that same power of music to help heal ourselves.

Aldous Huxley wrote that music's greatest potency lies in expressing the inexpressible. Grief often brings much time alone to deal with our feelings and our loss. What has worked for me is surrounding myself with music that is singing to me the words I need to hear or playing the notes and rhythms that reverberate through my being and bring me comfort. One day I'll be listening to silky soul music like Ron and I used to dance to, and the lyrics seem to be what I needed to hear at that moment. Another day I'll spend hours with baroque music playing in the background with memories of all the *Carmel Bach Festival* Jacques and I attended enjoying sumptuous food and glorious music. Now, I listen to many genres of music and have gained a love for the comfort it brings. I love Michael Franti with his love songs mixed in with his protest songs making me feel a little better about the world and causing me to think of more than just myself.

Music provides companionship. Some people keep the television on to have noise, but I prefer music when I am by myself because I can play what speaks to me at that moment. I can listen, or I can sing along, or I can even talk to the singer, any of which can make me feel less alone. Another great time to use music is when you meditate. Meditating at least daily has multiple benefits. Sometimes people resist meditation because they feel it is difficult to do, but when you add music to the meditation, you can be amazed by the depth you can go and the peace you can feel. You can find meditation apps for your phone or meditation mixes on YouTube, or you can find peaceful music that works for you. The best music for meditation is instrumental, without words. You can meditate sitting peacefully, or you can do a walking meditation with headphones. Both methods can be effective. Allow the music to exist without focusing on it. I struggled as I first was learning how to meditate, but the right music made all the difference for me. I am sure it can also help you.

I recall many times when I used music for motivation. For one theater production I acted in, I played the Pointer Sisters' song, *I'm So Excited*, every night as I drove to the theater, and when I got there, I was all revved up and ready to perform. When I directed a play about Hospice, I heard J. S. Bach's *Air on a G String* and I knew it was the music of the show. I played it as I prepared to direct and on breaks during rehearsal. It was so perfectly enhanced and supported the production. I also like to put on music while I am cooking, like Italian music for Italian food, Blues for a BBQ, or carols for baking Christmas cookies. When I use music for background, like when I am writing, I always choose instrumental music, and when I use music for companionship, I choose something upbeat with fun lyrics. Apps like Pandora, Spotify™, or Amazon™ music will let you choose a category to suit your mood and accompany your activities.

Tony Falzono says:

"Music is non-judgmental and never asks too much of you. Music states the obvious where words are difficult to speak. You don't have to entertain it, and its feelings aren't hurt when you tune it out or shut it off. Music is available anytime to act as a reliable companion."

Music is a great companion to have! I encourage you to take some time to figure out what music can best support you in feeling better. Find different songs for different moods and let your feelings guide you. One thing to keep in mind when you are looking for soothing music is to pick something with a rhythm similar to your heartbeat which can help you to sync up with the music. Also, try listening to music you aren't familiar with. Be willing to discover music from different cultures, eras, and styles. There are drums from Africa, and Gregorian chants from centuries ago. Hip Hop, Reggae, Classical, Techno, Instrumental, and even music with birds, whales, frogs, rain, and ocean waves. The options are infinite.

Once you find some music you like, begin creating music playlists that can help you focus on different areas of reclaiming your joy. Try looking up songs on YouTube for some inspiration. You can even create your own playlists there for free that you can listen to and add to any time you like. There are dozens of apps and music online for you to choose from. Pick the one that best suits you.

Choosing the Right Music For You

Here are some suggestions to get you started. Consider why and when you will be listening to the music to give you some ideas for categories. Create lists that:

* **Remind you of your loved one.**
  * What was your favorite song to listen to together?
  * What music did they enjoy and appreciate?
  * What songs bring forth the feelings that they inspired in you?
  * What songs are meaningful for you?
  * Are there songs that trigger favorite memories you have?
  * Do you have a song that resonates with your life or relationship?
  * Are there songs that always make you smile or bring you tears?
  * Do certain songs remind you of a special occasion or a place you visited?
* **Songs that comfort you.**
  * Are there songs you listen to that help you sleep?
  * Are there songs that you listen to because you know they will lift your mood?
  * Are there songs that bring you special memories?

I asked my Facebook group to suggest songs they would listen to deal with loss, and they were full of good suggestions. Try asking your friends for suggestions of songs that could bring you joy, comfort, or support. My group suggested:

* *You'll Never Walk Alone*, by Oscar Hammerstein II and Richard Rodgers, was Shirley's suggestion
* Anything Baroque, like Bach and Mozart, are Peach's favorites
* Nancy loves *It is Well with My Soul*, by Philip Bliss and Horatio G Spafford
* *Tell Your Heart to Beat Again* by Danny Gokey was suggested by Rev. Rachel Hollander
* *Through the Veil,* which was written and performed by Rev. Rachel Hollander

These songs led me on a search for songs that would be meaningful at the time of dealing with loss and searching for joy, and I discovered so many perfect songs. I suggest you listen to them all! You can find them in places like iTunes™, Pandora, Spotify™, Amazon Music, and YouTube.

* *Like a Star*, Corrine Bailey Rae
* *We're New Here*, Gil Scott-Heron and Jamie xx
* *When I Get There,* Pink
* *Tonight's the Night*, Neil Young
* *See You Again*, Carrie Underwood
* *Supermarket Flowers*, Ed Sheeran
* *Wake Me Up When September Ends*, Green Day
* *Everybody Hurts*, R. E. M.
* *Who You'd Be Today*, Kenny Chesney
* *When I am Gone*, Joey and Rory
* *Fire and Rain*, James Taylor
* *See You Again*, Wiz Khalifa
* *Will the Circle Be Unbroken*, Nitty Gritty Dirt Band
* *Tears in Heaven*, Eric Clapton
* *If Heaven Was Needing A Hero*, Jo De Messina
* *If I Die*, The Band Perry
* *I Grieve*, Peter Gabriel

* *Let it Be*, The Beatles
* *Dance With My Father,* Luther Vandross
* *Let's Hurt Tonight*, One Republic
* *You Were Loved*, Whitney Houston
* *Paradise*, Coldplay
* *Until Heaven*, Sarah Bertola
* *I'll Be Missing You*, Puff Daddy
* *Photograph*, Ed Sheeran
* *In the Arms of an Angel*, Sarah McLachlan
* *My Immortal*, Evanescence
* *Bridge Over Troubled Water*, Simon and Garfunkel
* *To Where You Are*, Josh Groban
* *I Lived,* One Republic
* *Til It Happens to You*, Lady Gaga
* *One More Light*, Linkin Park
* *One Sweet Day*, Maria Carey and Boyz ll Men
* *My Father's Eyes*, Eric Clapton
* *Adagio for Strings Opus ii*, Samuel Barber
* *Mourning Song,* Rickie Byars
* *Just Like That*, Bonnie Raitt

Take some time to listen to music and allow it to bring forth the very emotion you need to feel. Escape in it. Be inspired by it. Revel in it and find new joy and happiness there.

PRACTICE: CREATE YOUR PLAYLIST

Consider all the songs of your life that you have heard and that have created a feeling inside of you. Make a list of your favorites and divide them into categories like music that makes me happy, songs with great memories, or your loved one's favorite songs. Choose one of your lists, the one that speaks to you the most, and create a playlist to suit your mood. You can create it in an app like iTunes, or you can create your own playlist on YouTube where you can select the songs and videos you enjoy and have them available to listen to whenever you want.

KEY TIPS FOR CHAPTER NINETEEN

* Music inspires joy.
* Music can be soothing, comforting, supportive, and healing.
* Music helps you remember and connect to times in your life.

TAKE ACTION

HAPPINESS HABITS

Your Intention

* Write an *Intention* about how you are incorporating more music into your life.

I intend to _____

_____

_____

_____

_____

Your Gratitude

* *What are your three favorite songs?* Write why you are *grateful* for each of them.

I am happy and grateful that _____

_____

_____

_____

_____

Your Happiness

* Listening to music with a friend or friends can be a *happy* experience. Invite someone to listen to music with you. *Who will you invite? What music will you listen to?*

Your Affirmation

* Write a *positive affirmation* related to music, then live that affirmation.

I am _____

PERSONAL NOTES

PERSONAL NOTES

CHAPTER 20

PLAYING

"Fall in love with your own life."
—REV. JOANNE COLEMAN

Playing is the fastest, easiest way to reclaim your joy, and the benefits will last you a lifetime! Kristin Wong tells us in a New York Times article: *Play is similar to meditation in that it helps you focus on where you're at in the moment and reset your busy, perpetually exhausted adult mind.* Play is the process of letting go and being willing to feel confident, powerful, fulfilled, loving, and happy! Play brings you joy, it also brings you feelings of exhilaration, stimulation, rejuvenation, and relaxation! I want all these feelings, and I am sure you do also. And, I can hear you thinking, "I haven't played in forever," or "Playing is for kids." Let me share that playing is for everyone, and you can do it!

The feeling of joy comes from within and often it is sparked by doing something playful and fun. Someone or something else can't make you feel joy, but you can discover your own joy by focusing on the bright side of your life; by being playful. Especially when dealing with loss, we can get lost in our thoughts of how sad we are, how much we miss our loved ones, and how things will never be the same. While all those things may be true, you don't have to dwell in that mindset. Consciously shift your thinking into a positive mode. Instead of thinking about sad things, think about something that will make you happy. If talking to a special friend makes you happy, call them. If eating luscious food at your favorite café brings you joy, call a friend to go with you and enjoy! Add some fun to it and see how much it will improve your mood.

WHY PLAY IS SO IMPORTANT

If play is eluding you, take a deep look at yourself from an outside perspective. Remember that you are doing the best you can, that you are perfect, and that you already have what you are looking for. As Whitney Houston's song says: "I found the greatest love of all inside of me." Enjoy that love. Treat yourself the way you would honor and treat the person you love most because that is you, and that is how your loved one would want you to treat yourself. When you find that place inside yourself, you are able to let go and play. Play helps you open yourself to celebration and feel inner self-love!

Consider the many benefits of playing:

* **Play fosters creativity.** Playing activates the right side of the brain that stimulates creativity. When we play we concentrate on what we are doing—on dancing, singing, or however you like to play. This allows you to shut off the logical thoughts and stimulate creativity.

* **Play fuels your imagination.** *Remember all the stories you created when you played as a child?* You can do that in your life right now. I had an imaginary friend I always had fun with when I was little. You can do something like that where you have a best friend who will always enjoy the same things you do. Activate your imagination by being more playful when you can.

* **Play can help you solve problems.** Try to take things less seriously and use light-hearted and playful responses and reactions when problems arise. People around you will feel more relaxed when you see the funny side of a situation and use that to solve any issues.

* **Play helps you with emotional well-being.** If you start feeling down, try bouncing a ball outside, playing catch with a neighborhood child, or going swimming where you can relax and improve your emotional equilibrium.

* **Playing helps you be social.** Invite a friend to play tennis, go for a walk, or to put a puzzle together with you. Find a class to take where you can meet people, play, and be creative. Being playful gives you all kinds of reasons to make new friends and spend time with existing ones.
* **Play improves your brain function.** As the old saying goes, you lose it if you don't use it. Think of play as a mental exercise to keep that brain strong! Playing requires the brain to be active and you want a healthy brain.
* **Play relieves stress**. When you start feeling uptight, actively do something to release that tension by being playful. Go for a walk and try skipping, whistling, or wearing a funky hat or flower in your hair. Explore somewhere local you haven't been to before, like an amusement park, a botanical garden, or a park where you can relax or maybe even fly a kite. Let fun help you feel more at ease and calm inside because you are doing something you enjoy.

When you decide to play, allow yourself to completely immerse yourself in what you are doing. Keep it as unstructured as possible so that you don't worry about rules. Doing things that bring you joy feels so good when you add play and fun to it! Be willing to do something you love or find the joy in doing something new. Find things to do that you have always wanted to do that are playful and unconventional. No one said life has to be serious, so go do whatever it is that feels playful. Don't wait or hesitate. Go do it now.

When you are absorbed in playing, your senses are heightened, and you naturally flow into the present moment feeling awake and ready for whatever comes your way. I watched my neighbors' puppies playing, and they were wild in their activity, jumping, running, and playing with toys without a thought in the world. I want to play like that, having fun for the sake of fun. Research shows that animals that play the most live longer, and I am sure that also holds true for people.

I love Albert Einstein. My favorite quote of his is, "Imagination is more important than knowledge." When you think about it, all that he discovered came from playing with ideas until he discovered how they worked. When you play, when you are open to new things, when you experiment with the best way to do what you are doing, you are, in a sense, creating your own new life. As your life begins anew, be sure to include play to help you live in a state of joy, recognizing the good and beauty of everything, and always focusing on the positive.

PLAY FUELS THE BRAIN

Scientists have discovered that the brain actually has neurochemicals, hormones, and neurotransmitters that trigger happiness.[5] Stephanie Watson, the Former Executive Editor of *Harvard Women's Health Watch,* says in her article, "Feel-good hormones: How they affect your mind, mood, and body": *One group of hormones are nicknamed the "feel-good hormones" because of the happy and, sometimes, euphoric feelings they produce.* These discoveries are proof that your joy physically comes from inside of you. Yes, external factors can affect how you feel, but your brain is always working to make you happy. All you have to do is play along! Your brain actually changes based on your activities so why not make them fun?

When comparing the brains of people who participate regularly in different activities, scientists discovered that people doing the same activities reflect the same changes in their brains, like the brains of people who meditate, have similar changes, Brain changes are also similar in people who have had traumatic experiences. The research shows that our brains can change based on what we do. There are many ways to use scientific information to help you have more joy in your life. Try these ideas:

Every day, notice the good things around you. You can write a list to reinforce remembering what you discover. Allow yourself to feel the joy that comes from having a playful attitude. Often, we get in our own way, so instead of talking yourself out of feeling joy, talk yourself into experiencing the joy you seek. Do things specifically to bring you joy and see how much better you quickly feel.

---

[5] https://www.health.harvard.edu/mind-and-mood/feel-good-hormones-how-they-affect-your-mind-mood-and-body

EXAMPLES OF PLAY

When you start focusing on living, being, and experiencing playfulness, your body will then adapt to living in a more joy-filled state. Seek out fun ways to be more playful so that you shift from grieving to living life. Here are a few ideas:

* Taking a class
* Cooking
* Learn to play an instrument
* Drawing or painting
* Singing
* Gardening
* Dancing
* Starting a group to play board games together
* Creating a gourmet group to plan a dinner to cook together each month
* Creating a group to try a new restaurant each month
* Finding someone to do a sport with, like tennis, swimming, or golf
* Volunteering to work with children
* Volunteering at a charity
* Start a book club
* Hiking, camping, or being outdoors
* Adopting a pet

Though you can play by yourself, much of playing involves being social, so grab a friend and have a good time with them. When you play, you will discover that it relieves stress and improves your mood and your outlook. Playing also improves your social skills and relationships. The stimulation of play keeps your energy up. The object is to relax, forget your worries, and have fun.

Laughing comes easier when it is shared with others. Think about the joy you feel when watching kittens play or watching babies laugh. Plan to experience joy throughout your day. Start by saying "joy" often, like "I find joy in the beautiful sunrise" or "Having my morning cup of coffee makes me joyful each time I smile at the luscious aroma." You'll discover that incorporating the word "joy" into what you say will bring you smiles. Actively seek out good things, like noticing when someone opens the door for a stranger or when a stranger smiles at you, and you smile back and say hi. Notice the beauty around you. I adore blue skies and blooming flowers. *What makes you smile?* Seek that out, whatever it is.

My artist friend Bambi says when she wants to play, she takes a meandering drive, pulls out her new autoharp to strum gospel music, or plays with her new craft of wood carving, which brings her joy.

My friend Rachel told me, "With my Dad, he role-modeled for me how to always enjoy life, every little thing (because there are no little things). So, if I see a rainbow, I pull the car over to look at it because Dad said these were miracles. If there is carnival food somewhere, I break my "diet rules," and I eat something I haven't tried before! I like to sing and let the music play as often as possible!"

Look around at the people you know and ask yourself, *Who in your life inspires you to play and have fun?* Mirror others who make play important and follow their lead. Allow yourself to play and have fun. When we experience loss, often we feel an obligation to not smile or have fun, that somehow smiling disrespects our loved one who died—it does not. You deserve joy. Opening up to positive experiences will go a long way in helping you reclaim that joy. The more joy you experience, the more you will attract and notice it becoming part of your well-being.

Start fostering joy by setting yourself up for positive adventures. I knew I'd find joy by going to a Michael Franti concert. He is a singer who is all positive and loves love. In his concerts, he goes throughout the audience to be close to as many people as he can. His joy is infectious, and you can't help but jump, dance, and sing along. I went with three friends, and we still talk about how much fun we had. Plan some positive adventures for yourself. Take friends when you can, but don't hesitate to play by yourself.

Today is the day to start playing! Make a plan, and fully enjoy yourself.

Practice: Play!

Start by making a list of things you want to do to be more playful. Think about who you would like to do playful activities with. Then create a plan on how to activate and integrate that play into your life. It doesn't have to be complicated or exact. In fact, most play is spontaneous and unfolds when the intention for play is present. Let joy and play also come to you. Embrace when others want to be playful around you and be willing to let yourself loose. Do at least one playful thing on your list, then write about the experience in your journal. *Do you want to do that playful thing again? Or would you like to experiment with different ways to play?* Have fun!

Key Tips for Chapter Twenty

* Discover what activities bring joy into your life.
* Find activities you would like to try that foster play.
* Regularly incorporate play into life with an action plan.

Take Action

HAPPINESS HABITS

Your Intention

* Write an *Intention* about how you are incorporating play into your life each day this week.

I intend to _____

_____

_____

_____

Your Gratitude

* Write your three favorite ways to play and why you are *grateful* for them.

I am happy and grateful that _____

_____

_____

_____

_____

Your Happiness

* Get together with a friend or with friends who you find yourself *happy* with when you are with them and plan a way you can play together on a regular basis.

Then do it!

_____

_____

_____

_____

_____

Your Affirmation

* Write a *positive affirmation* that proclaims how you play.

I am _____

_____

_____

_____

_____

_____

_____

_____

CHAPTER 21

THE SLOWING OF TEARS

"Even the deepest pain will pass."
–MARK NEPO

You will notice that over time your tears will slow down—you may have days or weeks without them. Then they may pop up at the most inconvenient times; that's okay. Release them without judgment. The veil of tears we walk through with loss lightens, but it is there to serve you when you need it; when you have to cleanse your emotional storage and let go. Like a warm shower, tears can feel good, and the freshness you feel after they are shed can help you carry on with your day.

After I got home from the hospital where Jacques was officially pronounced dead it suddenly hit me that he was gone. Even though I knew the moment he was getting in the car and he slumped into his seat that his life had ended, the news from the hospital made it undeniably official. After I got home and was sitting on the couch with my friends Yvonne and Jan, I started to sob deep, uncontrollable tears wrenching up from the center of my being. I couldn't keep my eyes open. I felt like I couldn't breathe, gasping between sobs, and I couldn't seem to stop. I don't know how long I sobbed, but it eventually slowed. I began to feel empty. I couldn't talk. All I could do was sit. I had that empty feeling for days, afraid to start to cry again because of fear I wouldn't stop, yet finally, I did. I still had tears escaping at times, but I intentionally held myself back from fully crying for fear of falling back into the depths of those deep uncontrollable sobs.

When Ron died, it was so different. I was surrounded by people who loved him, we knew what was coming, and we had left nothing unsaid. I knew he was ready, but when he took his last breath, my sobs arrived. Thankfully our good friend Michelle was there with me and walked me to my bedroom, where I lay on the bed, and she held me as I cried. If anything, the crying was even longer and deeper than it had been before. Though I cried intermittently for a long time, I focused on remembering all the love and joy we shared, which helped me move through the tears so much.

I have witnessed much sobbing by others at the time of death. When I worked as a nurse, I could handle anything with caring for a patient, but if I had to give bad news to a family, I would fall apart after I told them, as their sobs were so hard to witness. To make sense of the crying, I turned to research and learned that there are different kinds of tears. We have some tears specifically to provide moisture, comfort, and protection to our eyes, while the tears that come with sadness, or emotional tears, have a different chemical make-up and actually can help us to feel better after crying. Knowing about the different kinds of tears helped comfort me when tears came, knowing that they were there for my own good and healing.

CRYING IS INFLUENCED BY CULTURE

The way we cry may be culturally influenced. I grew up with a father who would become easily emotional and cry for joy and celebration as well as for loss. My mother, on the other hand, would be embarrassed by his tears, and the first time I remember her crying in my life was when she heard me talking on the phone with her doctor, and I had to tell her that she had a brain tumor. We held each other and cried together for a long time. That was the first and last time I saw her cry.

The influence of my parents made me feel that crying wasn't acceptable, so if I did cry, I needed to do it in private. Fearing disapproval from Mom, I held back my tears for many years while I was growing up. My hope is that crying is much easier for you and you were raised around a family comfortable with tears. Tears are natural and every person on the planet is equipped to express tears during emotional times. In some cultures, crying is accepted, and mourning is expected to go on for years. How and when you cry may be heavily influenced by how and where you were raised, and there is no physical right or wrong way to cry.

Often people hold back tears after a death, especially in public, perhaps in fear of being seen as weak. Or they may not be comfortable with feeling out of control when crying. The lack of crying is often associated with not dealing with death. One of my group members told us how her mother died when she was young, and she hadn't cried then or for years after, but something triggered her one day, and she sobbed for what seemed like a lifetime. She described that when her tears stopped, she felt lighter, like she had been relieved of a burden she didn't realize she was carrying. Not crying when someone dies can act like a dam with pressure building up behind it to the point that eventually must break, and with it comes the relief from all the force that is released. On the opposite end of the spectrum, some people don't cry at all. Everyone handles their tears differently. Not everyone will react in the same way to the same situation; therefore, what is important is to not judge yourself or someone else for reactions.

Tears can be triggered by a variety of things, like being with others who are crying. I am a sympathetic crier. When I am with someone who cries, I will most likely be crying along with them. Or, you may cry when you see something that reminds you of your loved one or an experience you had together. More often than not, when I see a picture of Ron or Jacques, I smile and remember the good times, but other times when I see their smiles, I cry. Jacques died in our new car. I thought I would be okay with that, but it wasn't long before I realized that I had to sell it. The memories were too painful for me to deal with. Ron died at home in an area we had set up for him to use as his office. After he died, I had it painted and rented it to Robin, a dear friend. I love having her live close by, and I am able to remember good thoughts when I am in her apartment, and how Ron's death was so peaceful as he was surrounded by people who loved him.

YOUR TEARS ARE FOR YOU

You may be wondering, *how long will you find yourself crying?* That question doesn't have a specific answer, but these two examples may help you know that time is not what is important, it is how you feel. I recently went to a concert to see Michael Franti, my all-time favorite entertainer whose songs and heart fill the world with love. He talked about the tragedy of frequent school shootings that occur and how he went to be with the survivors of the Parkland, Florida shooting to support them. While he was there, a teacher invited him into her classroom, where they were studying the Nazi concentration camps. A survivor who was in his nineties and had lost his entire family while he was interned was the guest speaker that day. One of the students asked him how he was able to deal with that, and the man said he cried. He cried for over a year, all the time, every day. Then one day, the tears were gone—he realized he had survived, at that point, he also realized it was time for him to live.

Ellis, my trainer, reflected on his mother's death. He had a hard time dealing with his loss and ended up in the hospital for panic attacks for seven years after she died. The last time he was signing himself out from the hospital and he was asked to sign and date a form, he realized that it was the seventh anniversary of his mother's death and that it was the exact same date and time. At that point, he realized that he was okay and that she was also. He was finally able to release the constant sorrow.

Other people seem to recover more quickly. Four months after her husband died, Betty told me that she wasn't crying anymore and that she felt at peace. She thought maybe something was wrong with her, but I assured her that she had cried as much as she needed to. Her husband had been ill and was older, and his death seemed to her to be the best outcome for the situation. Each of our experiences is different for every person, every time, so expect to have different reactions.

The number of tears you cry, the number of days, weeks, months, or years that you cry, are your personal experience and reaction to your loss, and whatever your timeline is, that is the perfect timeline for you. The end of your tears doesn't signal the end of your loss. You will always miss your loved one, but over time grieving will take up less space as your life moves along. In that space, you will find room for joy as your loved one would want it for you. Live the rest of your life like you are ready for when the time comes for you, and find joy in every moment.

PRACTICE: JOURNAL YOUR TEARS

In your journal, write about your experience with crying. *How much have you cried? Do you still cry about your loss? How do you feel when you are crying? How do you feel when you stop crying?* Now that you know the difference between emotional tears and tears that your body creates for lubrication and health, *can you tell the difference in your tears when you cry? Do you feel like you have not cried enough or that you cry too much? Have your tears slowed?* Fully express yourself about your relationship with your tears.

KEY TIPS FOR CHAPTER TWENTY-ONE

* Crying is good for you.
* Two different kinds of tears exist.
* Your tears will slow down over time.

TAKE ACTION

HAPPINESS HABITS

Your Intention

* Write an *Intention* that supports your tears when they come.

I intend to _____

_____

_____

_____

_____

Your Gratitude

* Write about someone you are *grateful* for who has comforted you when you had tears.

I am happy and *grateful* that _____

_____

_____

_____

_____

Your Happiness

* Tears come when you are happy as well as sad. Write about a time you remember having *happy* tears. I still tear up when I think of how happy I was when my children were born. Cherish those tears.

_____

_____

_____

_____

_____

Your Affirmation

 * Write a *positive affirmation* supporting the value of the tears you cry.

I am _____

_____

_____

_____

_____

_____

CHAPTER 22

HELPING OTHERS IN THEIR GRIEF

*"Grief is like the ocean; it comes on waves ebbing and flowing.
Sometimes the water is calm, and sometimes it is overwhelming.
All we can do is learn to swim."*
–VICKI HARRISON

When we are grieving, we often find ourselves in the company of others who are also grieving and sometimes find ourselves at a loss of what to say. We have all had well-meaning people say something they thought would be comforting to us, but often what they say ends up being hurtful in some way. I am often asked by the people I work with what is the best thing to say when someone is grieving. There are many different answers you can give, and being prepared with what to say can help you recognize their grief and honor your own.

Here are some ideas to think about before you are faced with supporting someone else who may be grieving. Being prepared can help you avert your own tears that may arise as you attempt to comfort someone else. When you speak with love and caring, people can recognize the kinship that can come from grieving together.

Saying the right things to someone who is grieving can be a challenge. In the awkwardness following a death, sometimes people don't know what to say, so many times they don't say anything, and I guarantee, that is not helpful. Someone will most likely say, "I'm sorry for your loss," hoping to be compassionate. I remember years ago when the phrase, "Have a nice day," suddenly became popular. When you parted company with anyone, they would likely say, "Have a nice day." At first, I thought that was pleasant for people to do until it became a constant response that lost its meaning. That's where "I am sorry for your loss" is currently; it is said with little true understanding. People seem to think that any time they hear someone has died, those words must be spoken out of courtesy before anything else is said. I've heard "I'm sorry for your loss," said like ordering fries with a meal. It sounds absurd, but that is a habit people have begun doing without realizing the impact of their words. Saying those words does not help anyone except maybe for the person saying them that feels they are doing it out of obligation.

I heard a veteran say that she felt the same way about "Thank you for your service." She said, "If that person was so grateful, they could give me a job, and then I'd feel grateful." I have heard that for military personnel and veterans, the better thing to say is "Never forget." I like that. If someone said something like, "I'll never forget Ron and what a special person he was," I would appreciate that heartfelt thought.

Don't let your discomfort get in the way of showing up for your friend who needs you. With society's attitude toward death, it's easy to run the other way when it occurs, but that doesn't help your friend who is experiencing the worst time of his or her life right now, and it doesn't help you. Step up, be brave, and do what you can for your friend—you may not need to say anything. Just listen and be supportive.

WE CAN BE SUPPORTIVE

There are many things to consider when deciding how to best express your condolences to someone else who is grieving. The primary thing is to speak from your heart not from what we see on TV or hear in the movies. When what you say comes across as flip or thoughtless, or if you say something that you know is not in line with the beliefs of the person you are trying to comfort, what you say may do more harm than good. Since this chapter is about how to help others who are experiencing grief, I invite you to see how you can find ways to support them in the same way you need support.

I know that you likely have been dealing with things people have said to you, and you could probably make a list of your own comments that hurt more than they healed. My list here is a gentle reminder of things to avoid so that you don't help people to feel worse versus better.

Here's a list of things I suggest *not* to say to someone who is grieving and dealing with loss. These statements can sometimes be misinterpreted and feel hollow in their intent.

* **"I am sorry for your loss."**
    * Instead, *what could you say that shows you are thinking about the person who died and that you want the griever to feel better?*
* **"He (or she) is in a better place."**
    * Unless you are sure of the belief system of who you are talking to, talking about a "better place" may not be appropriate at all. Or, that person may be hurt by knowing that the place where that person was, in the loving home and arms of the person you are talking to, was a pretty special place that would be hard to leave.
* **"Look for the bright side."**
    * Generally, there is no bright side to death. A person may no longer be suffering, but that doesn't ensure brightness.
* **"I know how you feel because I lost a pet."**
    * Now I know we love our pets dearly, but a pet is not a parent, child, or friend. People are likely to be hurt when someone compares their loved one to an animal.
* **"What you need to do now is . . . ."**
    * Grieving is enough for someone to do. Don't make them feel like they have homework from you. You don't want them to feel guilty about not doing what you suggest."
* **"Time heals all wounds."**
    * The person grieving is dealing with the present moment and may not be able to even consider their future without their loved one.

* **"If only you would have taken them to the doctor sooner, maybe they would still be alive."**
    * We can't change the past, don't foster regret. As hard as it is to believe, people do say thoughtless words. Don't be one of them.
* **"You can always have another child (or find another husband/wife)."**
    * One does not replace the other. The person who died was a unique person that could not be replaced.
* **"At least he/she had a long life."**
    * *What difference does that really make?* The person is still gone, and having someone in your life for a really long time may make it even harder to grieve.
* **"They brought those health issues onto themself."**
    * If only they wore sunscreen, didn't eat or drink so much, or went to the gym. After someone dies, none of these types of things make any difference, so don't bring it up.
* **"You have to stay strong."**
    * Early grief can be the weakest, most vulnerable part of someone's life, so don't encourage something that may not be possible. Overcoming grief is not about strength.

I could go on and on with other examples, but I know you understand as you may have had some things said in your grieving that are hard to understand. I am amazed at the inappropriate things that people say due to not knowing or having any experiences with grief. It is a great exercise to write in your journal some things that people have said to you that weren't helpful. Knowing what *not* to say can be a guide for you when the time comes for you to comfort someone else. Now that you are in the position of someone who has lost a loved one, you will discover, if you haven't already, that some people will consider you somewhat of an expert because of what you have been through. They will seek guidance from you. Here is a list of things that will be good for you to express to them:

* Acknowledge the pain. People grieving often feel like they are the only one who has ever hurt so deeply. Tell them that their pain is real, that we all experience it at times in our lives, and let them know that you would be happy to listen.

* Tell them that you don't know what to say and that you care, and you love them.
* Tell them the favorite thing you remember about the person who died: their smile, their laugh, and the events that you shared. Tell them anything positive you remember.
* Let them know you will listen, then listen without judgment or advice. Sometimes we need to express what we are feeling and know someone hears us.
* Tell them if you would be happy to come to stay with them for a few days or longer.
* Ask them to talk to you about their loved one any time they want.
* Tell them that they don't have to talk, that you will sit by them and be there for them.
* Tell them you are so sorry that they have to go through such a big loss.
* Let them know that they are in your prayers.
* Remind them there is no 'right' way to grieve. Everyone does their own unique process that is best for them.

There are many things you can say to someone who is grieving, The best is to express yourself from the heart. Trust that you will know what to say when the time arrives. Be honest, be kind, be loving, and the best words will come to you. Keep in mind that when you are expressing yourself or offering advice that what you say needs to be about the person you are talking to. I had several people say to me something like: "I don't know what I would do if I had two husbands die. If I had one die, that would be bad enough, but having two die must be awful." They really did say this, truly out of lack of information and not understanding grief. Be sure to think about what you want to express before you say it. If it's not helpful and can't be said with love, it is better not to speak.

Do be careful with religious comments or references. I have heard people throw around comments about what God would want or do, and these things can actually be harmful depending on the person you are talking to. If you know their beliefs and can relate to them in a way you both are comfortable with, by all means, say what you can which can be of the deepest comfort. If you don't know, however, you may accidentally say something that can be of the deepest hurt. Therefore, be cautious to express things from your heart with love.

HELPING THEM THROUGH IT

When you are dealing with someone who is also grieving, what else can you do to help? My best answer is: pick something specific. Please don't say, "Just let me know if you need anything." They aren't going to call you, or if they do, it's likely to be at a point where they really need you right then and you may not be available. Instead, be proactive. Take them food, flowers, or little gifts weeks or months after the death. Let them know they are remembered. If you are taking food to someone who lives alone, a giant casserole is not a good idea, but that casserole divided into individual servings and wrapped for the freezer would be much appreciated.

Sometimes we let our fear hinder us from doing what we would like to or what we think is best. Don't let fear get in your way. Go to your friend and offer to listen, offer to help, offer to be there. Offer to do practical things like laundry, housework, or yard work. When friends and family gathered at our home while Ron was on hospice, our friend Maggie took over being sure that everyone had something to eat. I didn't even think about food at that time until everyone was gone, but when I realized what she had done, I was so grateful.

Remember to keep supporting your friend when all the celebrating is over, and everyone goes home. They may appreciate your presence for weeks, months, or a lifetime. You don't need to sacrifice what you do in your life, but you can be a good friend and love and support each other. One of the things I do is send a note every week for a year to a friend who has lost a loved one. I've been told that a little something in the mail is a reminder of love, and support has helped a great deal.

When you are grieving, you often have others around you who are also grieving. When you are helping a grieving friend for the long haul after a loss, be aware if you see signs of depression, like:

* Difficulty functioning in daily life
* Extreme focus on the death

* Excessive bitterness, anger, or guilt
* Neglecting personal hygiene
* Alcohol or drug abuse
* Inability to enjoy life
* Withdrawing from others
* Constant feelings of hopelessness
* Talking about dying or suicide

These are classic signs that you can find online or in a textbook. If you think that your friend has these signs, work with them to be seen by a doctor or counselor. Depression may be serious. And take any talk of suicide as something serious and that requires help right away. Call the National Suicide Prevention Hotline for guidance in the United States: 1-800-273-8255.

Other things you can do is to call when you are on your way out shopping to see if they'd like you to pick something up. You can invite them out for coffee or lunch or a walk, or help with some gardening. You may want to offer to come to watch a movie with them and bring popcorn, or have them over to your place to watch a movie. Pick up the phone to say I love you, or send a cute meme by email or a message.

The most important thing is to stay in touch. Share your love and support, and make the most of the special time you can share.

PRACTICE: A LETTER OF SUPPORT

Think of a friend who has recently been dealing with a loss. Write that friend a letter expressing the kind of support you would love to have had. Call their loved one by name, and include good memories. Tell them something that you will do to support them, like bring them dinner or drive them to appointments or call them every week, and then be sure to follow through and do what you offered. Be sure to mail the letter. Remember to write a new, personal letter each time a friend is dealing with a loss. The process of writing will provide comfort to your friend and to you as well.

KEY TIPS FOR CHAPTER TWENTY-TWO

* What *not* to say to someone grieving.
* What *to* say to those who are grieving.
* How you can help someone in grief.

TAKE ACTION

HAPPINESS HABITS

Your Intention

* Write an *Intention* expressing what you will always do for your friends and family when a loved one dies.

I intend to _____

_____

_____

_____

Your Gratitude

* Write three things you are *grateful* to do to help someone else deal with their loss.

I am happy and grateful that _____

_____

_____

_____

Your Happiness

* Remind yourself of the importance of *happiness* in your life. Write out a plan for nurturing yourself with happiness and explain how you will remind your friends to be happy.

_____

_____

_____

_____

_____

Your Affirmation

* Write a positive *affirmation* expressing the strength you have in helping others who are grieving.

I am _____

_____

_____

_____

_____

_____

Chapter 23:

Writing Letters

"When you get, give. When you learn, teach."
–MAYA ANGELOU'S GRANDMOTHER

L etter writing is becoming a lost art. As a child, I remember the beautiful handwriting that my mother and her sisters had. All the letters were perfectly shaped in a graceful script. They all had been taught so properly in school that I could not tell their handwriting apart from each other. My grandmother used a beautiful script, and some of my favorite treasures are letters she wrote. In her day, there were no computers or even phones, the only way to keep in touch was by writing. Letters have been a cherished item for many and one of the most heartfelt ways to communicate.

Throughout my life, I have treasured the letters I've received. Someone took the time to write to me and I love their sentiment. Letters are a reflection of the caring, respect, and love of the writer to the recipient. The process of writing letters can bring peace, relief, and love to those that write them, and appreciation, excitement, and thankfulness to those that receive them.

I have been a writer most of my life, and I have taught writing for many years at the university. When I was confronted with my husbands' deaths, the logical thing for me to do was write about them which led to me writing this book. After that, I started teaching *Writing Through Grief* classes and I discovered how much writing helps in the grieving process. Letter writing is my students' favorite exercise in class. We will write letters to those we are grieving. Then we write letters back to ourselves from who we wrote the initial letters to. We also write letters to our future selves or even to a Higher Power.

IMPORTANT LETTERS FOR YOU

I encourage you to try writing some of these letters to see what happens for you.

* **Write letters to be read by your children after you pass away.**
  * A beautiful example of letters to children was a young mother who knew she didn't have long to live and wouldn't be able to see her children grow up. She wanted her children to know how much she loved them, so she wrote birthday letters to them to be opened each year. In these letters, she told them the age-appropriate things she would like to have shared, gave them advice, and expressed her love. By writing these letters, she provided a way for her to always be remembered as a part of their lives.
* **If your children are older, write them a letter about a life lesson you have learned or your favorite memories of them.**
  * Reinforce things that are important to you and that you want others to know. Know that they will have a handwritten memory of the love you express for them. Share experiences you have had that they can learn from. Recall what worked in your life and what you wish you would have done more of or less of. Show them the importance of sharing love in their lives—let them know it is okay to be happy. Feeling guilty about finding joy or happiness after someone dies is not unusual. Show them that being happy is okay. Finding joy is important. Finding love is necessary.
* **Write a letter that can be used as a eulogy for your celebration of life.**
  * No one knows better than you what you would like to be remembered for. Include who and what you are most proud of.

Share your favorite memories and express your gratitude to those who have helped you along the way.

* **Write a love letter to yourself.**
    * We can be our own worst critics and enemies. Start by forgiving yourself for any guilt you may feel or transgressions you think you committed. When you are clear on your forgiveness, write all the things you love about yourself. *What are you proud of? What brings you joy?* Realize what makes you special. Know that the greatest love you can experience is your own.
* **Write letters to your loved ones who have died either recently or long ago.**
    * Write a heartfelt letter to them, talking to them the way you would if they were still alive. Express gratitude for everything you want to thank them for. Tell them your happiest, favorite memories together and what you do to remember them. Share anything you didn't get to say while they were still alive. Write it as a love letter if you like. Recall your favorite advice, and even ask them for some wisdom you can use now.
* **After you write a letter to your loved one, write a letter back to you from them.**
    * Start writing and let the words flow, not censoring what you write. You will be amazed at the answers you receive. Some people who have tried writing a reply believe that their loved one is dictating the letter, while others believe that they always had the answers inside themselves but didn't realize that until they wrote it out.
* **Write a holiday letter to family and friends.**
    * I had always written holiday letters to keep in touch with friends, but after Ron died, I wasn't sure I could write anything. I discovered that the process of writing a holiday letter the first year was the most helpful thing I did for myself in my grieving process. It helped me reflect on my experience of that year and all the beautiful things I had learned.

* Here is the sharing I put on my Christmas card the year Ron died: *"Christmas this year is a time of reflection for me. In a year of deep experiences, I've learned so much.*
  * *I learned the peace of living only in the moment.*
  * *I learned the joy of spending all my time with Ron.*
  * *I learned the love of being surrounded by our Ohana and loving friends and family.*
  * *I learned the gratitude we have for the perfect care given by Hospice.*
  * *I learned the beauty of Hawaiian culture in the memorial service for Ron on the Beach.*
  * *I learned the strength I didn't realize I have in looking forward to each new day.*

  This holiday season and next year, I wish you peace, joy, love, gratitude, beauty, and strength.
  Love,
  Emily, and Ron"

* **Write a letter to God or who or what you believe in.**
  * Pour out all of your feelings and ask all the questions you would love answers for. Take your time and say all you want to say. When you are finished, write a letter back to you from who you addressed your letter. Write what comes to you without question or judgment, and wait until you are finished writing before you read it. As I mentioned earlier, the answer comes from where you believe it does. It may come from deep within your heart or psyche or from your Higher Power. Wherever it comes from, it is likely to be filled with exactly what you need to hear.
* **Write letters to those people who have been helping you.**
  * I wrote letters to doctors, caregivers, neighbors, friends, family, and anyone who had been giving me help and support. Writing letters of gratitude was cathartic for me, leaving me feeling loved and at peace.

* **Write a letter to someone you know who is grieving.**
  * When our friend Chappy died suddenly while still young, I knew his wife Lori would be totally unprepared. As soon as I heard, I sat down and wrote her a long letter of love and advice on everything I could think of that she would be dealing with during the first couple of weeks. She was grateful, and I learned much for myself by writing the letter. A letter means so much more than a card.

You will discover times when writing a letter will be the perfect activity for you. I regularly write letters to Ron and Jacques on our anniversaries, birthdays, and Valentine's Day. Reminiscing with love and joy helps me from feeling down on those days that I am missing them. I also write letters to them when I am up against a challenge or a problem I can't solve. Writing out what's bothering me often brings me answers. I keep a special journal for these letters, and I refer to them at times when I am feeling a little lonely or when I am remembering them.

Other ideas of what to do with the letters you write are to put them in an envelope and seal them, maybe tie them together with a ribbon, or if you don't want anyone else to see what you wrote. You can then safely burn the letter if you like the idea of turning it into a ceremony. You can also opt to keep them on your bedside table or share it with a loved one you know would understand. Or you could start a blog posting letters to your loved one to help others who can learn from you. Your letters could be helpful to others who suffered a loss similar to yours.

WRITING YOUR STORY

Beyond writing letters, consider writing your life story for your loved ones to have. Ron's son Yusef asked his dad to write his story because he wanted to be able to share it with his son Jet as he grew up. For some reason, Ron resisted. I only got to be with Ron for the last ten years of his life, and of course, he had told me about experiences he had, but I didn't think to write them down at the time. After Ron died, I started writing what I could, but some memories were left with him. I have shared what I remembered with Ron's children, but I wished I could have shared more.

I am now working on a memoir about myself. I have started my memoir a couple of times in my life, but I found it got too detailed. Now I have a better perspective of what I want to include, especially my favorite memories that I feel others can learn from and I want to be remembered.

A good way to start writing your memoir is to create a framework. You may start with places you have lived, decades of your life, or even your relationships with people special to you. What you share can be used as a basic outline, then fill in each category with ideas you want to write more about. You will be amazed at how easily things come to you, and you might become amazed at who you have become, what you have done, or that you survived so much. Everyone's story is significant to those who love them, and what you write will be cherished.

WRITING YOUR WISHES

Something important to consider is writing the instructions or requests you'd like to happen after your death. You do need to have a will, a trust, and other legal documents, but beyond that, you may want to leave some explanations. I became my aunt's conservator before she died at her request. While she was competent, she told me what she wanted, and I agreed to take care of her in the way she desired. The problem was, she hadn't shared her desires with her son. While I could show him the legal documents that she had executed, he was furious with the decisions I had to make. We ended up in a painful court battle, and he hasn't spoken to me since she died. Had she written down her wishes, everything would have been so much easier. In your case, if you have done something like leave your estate to your favorite charity, please tell anyone affected by your decision while you still can. Including if you want to be cremated or not, if you want or do not want any kind of service, or if you don't want to be resuscitated if you stop breathing will not only bring you peace of mind, but will also give peace of mind to all those who will be affected.

Get out a pen and a notebook or journal or open up a file on your computer and start writing. Write often and write everything you want to remember and what you would love to have remembered about you. Establishing a writing practice will bring you much peace of mind.

Practice: Write

You have read many suggestions regarding writing. Choose one suggestion that resonates with you and write that. Then choose another one, and write that. These writing suggestions can be repeated as often as you would like. Consider getting together with friends to write, and then share with each other what you have written. Be sure to mail any letters you have written or burn the ones that will help you let go. Whenever you can, share your feelings in a letter to yourself or someone else you care about.

Key Tips for Chapter Twenty-Three

* The importance of sharing love via letters.
* Finding happiness and joy is healthy even while grieving.
* The value of remembering those you have loved.

Take Action

HAPPINESS HABITS

Your Intention

* Write a list of the letters you are *intending* to write including who you are writing them to.

I intend to _____

_____

_____

_____

Your Gratitude

* Reflect on letters you have written or received in your lifetime and why you are *grateful* for those letters.

I am happy and grateful that _____

_____

_____

_____

_____

Your Happiness

* Write about the *happiness* you anticipate that will come from the writing of each of these letters.

Then write about the happiness you experienced when you do write the letters.

_____

_____

_____

_____

_____

Your Affirmation

* Write a *positive affirmation* about the power of your words.

I am _____

_____

_____

_____

_____

_____

CHAPTER 24
WONDER, AWE, AND AMAZEMENT

"If you find your path, you are always on your way."
–LOUIS SCHWARTZBERGER, PHOTOGRAPHER

O pen your eyes and heart to wonder, awe, and amazement. I've been watching a big, giant full rainbow all morning, and I can't get enough of it. I revel in the beauty of where I live. I look up at the millions of stars I can see at night and realize the vastness of our universe. I admire my sparkly pink toenails with glitter and little hearts and smiles. I recall holding my babies in my arms and feeling more love than I realized could exist. I recall the first time I saw a Van Gogh original painting and I realized how he had seen through his eyes exactly what I was seeing right then. Life is full of wonder, awe, and amazement. We tend, however, to be so involved with our busyness that it often slips by unnoticed.

A moment of awe I experienced was at my wedding to Ron. As I gazed into his eyes, I was overcome with amazement that we had found each other and were so perfect together. I felt a real energy surge between us as we held hands. We felt like we were the center of the universe, held in a vortex of love. The feeling was an intense knowing of what love is and where we are meant to be. The wedding was outside, and breathing the fresh air was as if experiencing love rushing into us, then exhaling that love back at each other and to our intimate group of friends and family, and into the infinity of the universe and beyond. The rest of our lives together would be spent in the growing and blossoming of that experience, continuing to find more joy and more love. Yet, our wedding day was truly a magical feeling of awe and wonder I will remember forever.

We all have experienced wonder, awe, and amazement; however, those experiences often become muddled or lost as we keep being or doing what we think we should. I recall the miracle of pregnancy. When I first discovered that I was pregnant, I would lie on my back with my hands folded over my lower abdomen, overcome with the knowledge that a baby was growing inside of me. I could do that for hours. I knew right from the start that Jason was a boy and Abby was a girl, even though they didn't do sonograms in those days. When I started to feel their movements, I was overwhelmed with joy and tears, and was so grateful that I was blessed to have these experiences.

BEING IN AWE

Many of us have been blessed to have memorable and life-changing situations occur. Things happen every day that are tiny miracles at work. You may need to look beyond your circumstances and ask yourself, *When have you had such profound experiences?* Learn to be more in touch with what has been given to you by something greater than you.

I have been with family, friends, and strangers as they moved on from their mortal existence. At times it was fast and unexpected, like when I went on ambulance calls and picked up accident victims who were healthy and vital in one moment, and the next moment they were gone. These moments were accompanied by a shock when things didn't seem real. It was like I was in a pocket of time where I didn't quite fit. Other experiences were slower and more peaceful. Death arrives in all kinds of ways for us to process.

When my mother died, I was with her. She had a brain tumor and had been slipping away for months. She had stopped eating, lost weight, and was becoming weaker. I could hardly recognize her as the person she had been. I knew she was struggling to hold on, so I sat holding her arm and feeling her pulse. Knowing her beliefs, I talked to her and told her how happy Daddy and her Mother would be to see her. Shortly after I said that, her pulse slowed and then stopped. Being there at that moment, I sensed the profound difference in the room. I am grateful to have been part of her experience. I was also with Jacques, my Aunt Ila, Ron's mother Fran, and Ron when they crossed to the other side. These were the biggest moments of wonder, awe, and amazement I have ever had in my life.

Noticing Amazement

When I had my theater and school of arts, I remember a 12-year-old boy who was on the autism spectrum. He wouldn't look anyone in the eye, and though he often talked to himself, he rarely talked to others. By the end of our summer program, he was performing as the master of ceremonies for our show and telling jokes, loving to interact with the audience. Through the opportunity to perform, he opened up a part of him his parents had never seen before. Witnessing a small miracle was such a joy and reinforced for me why I created that school.

I also experienced amazement at hearing the story of a young woman from my neighborhood. My daughter is a volunteer ballroom dance teacher for differently-abled adults. When she met Anita, she had a beautiful smile and loved to dance though she had a great deal of trouble verbally communicating. After her dance training, Anitia's parents took her on a trip to Europe, and one night in a beautiful old hotel where they were staying, they had a ball, and Anita went with her parents. Most people there didn't speak English, but when a young man asked her to dance, she was all smiles. She wowed everyone with her dance skills and was literally the bell of the ball for the evening, with no one there having any idea that she was different from them. She experienced a real fairy tale dream come true.

Welcome in Wonder

Nature brings opportunities to experience naturally occurring phenomena deeply. On the island of Hawaii, the next island over from where I live, the volcano *Kilauea* erupted for months. We were captivated by the videos showing the eruptions. I always thought the lava shot out of the top of a triangular-shaped mountain, but the eruption split open the ground so the bright red lava would shoot high up into the air, destroying everything in its path and creating many new square miles of the island. As we watched, fascinated at a safe distance away, many homes and roads were covered with lava. Yet we all gathered to help those who lost everything, and we could feel the compassion of the prayers being said by so many people at once. There was a wonderful connection of so many people coming together in a powerful display of support.

Wonder and awe can also come at times of great tragedy. People around the world were struck when Notre Dame Cathedral burned as we all watched on our televisions, and we saw the people of France come together and spontaneously break into *Ave Maria* and other songs in solidarity. When disasters occur, people always rally to make donations of clothing, food, and money to be sent to total strangers suffering great loss. With the advent of programs like GoFundMe™, amazing amounts of money have been contributed to help people facing a huge variety of challenges, from paying for life-saving surgery to contributing to funerals for victims of violence. We love the feeling of being able to make a difference in wonderful ways.

Awe, Wonder & Amazement

Andrew Penn says[6], "Awe, it seems, reminds us that we are both grandly connected to a vast universe, and at the same time, delightfully insignificant, like a single star in a milky way." Experiencing wonder, awe, and amazement reminds us of the perspective of living. They show us that we are incredible physical organisms that can think, learn, grow, heal, love, and feel the joy of living. Consider your body for a moment. *What have you seen that took your breath away? What have you heard that vibrated through your body and made*

---

[6] https://www.hmpgloballearningnetwork.com/site/pcn/article/notre-dame-burning-grieving-loss-awe

you dance? What have you touched that was luxurious? What have you tasted that makes your mouth water just to think of it? When has your love been so big that it brought you tears of joy? Think of the blood cells coursing through your body while your heart continues to beat every moment. Consider how magnificent it is to take a deep breath. Notice a scar you have on your body from a cut or burn that healed perfectly. We don't have to search for wonder, awe, and amazement—we each live it every moment, especially when we take the time to pay attention.

What do you feel when you see a waterfall, a field of wildflowers, waves crashing to the shore, a giant whale and her calf frolicking in the ocean, or a newborn baby? What makes the hair on the back of your neck stand up, or what gives you goosebumps? Research has only started being done recently on the life-changing value of awe. In a 2012 study at Stanford University[7], researchers found that experiences of awe can increase your well-being and quality of life while helping you to anchor into the present moment. They discovered these four things about awe:

* **Awe can inspire creativity.** As amazing as it was to stand in the presence of Michelangelo's statue of David when I saw it in Florence, Italy, I was even more amazed by his unfinished sculptures on display. There were huge pieces of marble, which he would start carving from the front of the marble, allowing the image he was carving to emerge perfectly as he worked his way to the back of the figure. All of the art I witnessed in Tuscany amazed me, but Michelangelo's process had me longing for a home where I could get my hands into clay to see what sculptures would emerge.

* **Awe can give us hope and help us to appreciate life.** When I worked as a scrub tech in the obstetrics operating room, I never stopped getting blown away by the birth of a baby. Being there as the little bodies would feel air for the first time, as they took their first breaths and cried their first cries, never ceased to bring tears to my eyes and joy to my heart. I was always inspired knowing that each new little person was starting their grand adventure to see where life

---

[7] https://www.gsb.stanford.edu/faculty-research/publications/awe-expands-peoples-perception-time-enhances-well-being

would take them, and I still remember the feelings that came to me with each birth. And when babies were born with challenges, like deformities or conditions incompatible with living, their presence was a lesson in compassion for them, me, and their families.

* **Awe can connect us with nature.** Ron got up early each day to sit outside and start his day with God. We enjoyed so much time sitting outside and having long, meaningful conversations. When we lived close to the beach in California, we often had a fire burning in the chimenea, and in Maui, we'd enjoy the blue skies and bird songs. We found so much joy in all the different kinds of beauty on the islands, from the vortexes in *Iao* Valley to the trees in *Makawao* Forest, to the gentle waves of Sugar Beach, to the giant sea turtles of *Ho'okipa* Beach. I learned to love and value all my time outside in nature.

* **Awe can be transformative.** Psychologist Abraham Maslow developed a theory of Peak Experiences that could become life-changing. He felt that moments of Awe could remind us of how beautiful, good, and desirable the world is and that we could have these transcendent moments in simple experiences as well as with intense, big experiences.[8]

You have the opportunity to experience joy and transformation as you become aware of moments of wonder, awe, and amazement that surround you. Take the time to see where these things exist in your life. If you are having trouble identifying them, try asking others where they see awe, question where they feel amazement, or inquire about their wonder for new things or experiences. Seeing these through someone else's lens helps us fine-tune our own.

---

[8] https://www.pursuit-of-happiness.org/history-of-happiness/abraham-maslow/

PRACTICE: WONDERFUL MEDITATION

Find a beautiful, peaceful place where you can meditate quietly. As you meditate, breathe in slowly, focusing on wonder. Breathe out slowly, focusing on awe. Take your time with meditation, feeling the amazement of how your body functions, the beauty in nature surrounding you, and the wonder of love. Take time to meditate daily, and always include wonder, awe, and amazement as part of your meditation.

KEY TIPS FOR CHAPTER TWENTY-FOUR

* Every day, recognize the wonder around you.
* Every day, experience awe.
* Every day, be amazed.

TAKE ACTION

HAPPINESS HABITS

Your Intention

* Write an *Intention* about how you are going to pay attention specifically to the wonder, awe, and the amazement you experience in life.

I intend to _____

_____

_____

_____

_____

Your Gratitude

* Write what you are *grateful* for in relation to the experiences you have had with wonder, awe, and amazement.

I am happy and grateful that _____

_____

_____

_____

_____

Your Happiness

* Get together with a friend or friends and *have a conversation about wonder, awe, and amazement* in your lives, and talk about how these experiences made you happy.

_____

_____

_____

_____

Your Affirmation

* Write a *positive affirmation* about a way you can bring more to the lives of others.

I am _____

_____

_____

_____

_____

_____

_____

CHAPTER 25

REINVENTING YOURSELF THROUGH YOUR CLOSET

"If we can just let go and trust that things will work out the way they're supposed to, without trying to control the outcome, then we can begin to enjoy the moment more fully. The joy of the freedom it brings becomes more pleasurable than the experience itself."
–GOLDIE HAWN

*H*ow long has it been since you took a serious look at the clothes in your closet? *The books on your shelf? The items in your home, in storage, and outside in the garage.* Since you are going through a major transition in your life, it's time to begin releasing what feels no longer connected to you.

LETTING GO OF CLOTHING

I went to listen to my friends play music, and I looked at myself in a full-length mirror. I looked so different than I had the year before. I lost a lot of weight and had been building up muscle by going to the gym and walking. I smiled and felt good about how I was looking; then, I got dressed. The first dress I put on was so short. I remembered talking to Ron about that. Since I am so tall, finding dresses long enough for me was difficult. He would laugh and tell me how much he loved my long legs and that "length doesn't matter." Looking at myself in the mirror, I realized that length matters to me. When I would wear something longer, I didn't feel like I needed to wear shorts under my dress, and I actually felt more feminine, so right then I decided that it was time to start dressing in a way that made me feel good.

Piece by piece, I went through my closet and lovingly released anything that no longer served me. I didn't need to keep business attire since I live in Maui and would not have occasion to wear a suit. The long slacks that I would never wear again had to go. A snug pair of leggings would be ideal if I ever wanted to wear long pants because it was a little chilly. I no longer need cocktail attire because a sundress is perfect if I go out for a Mai Tai. My usual uniform is short-shorts and long, flowy tank tops, perfect for the island sun and trade winds, so there is no need to let them go.

The items I knew I would not need to wear again were easy to release. But the hard part was my dresses. Over the years, I had collected dresses when we would come to visit Maui before we decided to move here. Each dress had a memory. Usually, Ron and I were shopping together, and he would say things like how he really liked what I looked like in that dress. I tried on a dress from my closet, and I would recall how good it felt when I wore it when we danced together; then, I would notice how it was so short that it barely covered the short-shorts I would wear underneath. I knew that particular dresses would keep me stuck in the past, and I deeply needed a change to move forward. So, one by one, I tried on my clothes. I assessed each item by how I felt when I wore it, if it was still in style, if I would be comfortable wearing it, and if it was something I needed to keep for any reason. Examining each item, piece by piece, I ended up with lots more room in my closet.

I then had to decide what to do with all the items I was releasing. I shared many items with my friends. One friend suggested I take what was left to our favorite consignment store because they'd bring good prices, but that didn't work for me. I remembered how I took my mother-in-law's clothes to a consignment store and how even though I had no personal or sentimental connection to the clothes, I felt their judgment as they went through all I brought, saying things like "This is so out of style," or "No one would wear something like this." I made the decision that, in my case, the consignment store would not work for me. I could donate work clothes to *Dress for Success* to help give someone a fresh start. I decided other clothes could go to the women's shelter. I have to admit, there were some items I knew I wouldn't wear again, and I also knew I couldn't let them go yet. So, for now, I am hanging on to them until I know the best place to pass them on.

My friend Dawn works taking care of an older lady, cooking for her, getting her to appointments, and taking her shopping. The lady can afford anything she wants, and she loves to shop. After one of her first shopping trips, Dawn helped the lady hang her new purchases in her closet. She was running short of space and wondering where she would put it all. Dawn noticed that lots of the clothes still had tags hanging on them. They had never been worn. And the lady really didn't have any place to wear them all. As Dawn told me of her experience, I thought, "What a waste!" Then, the next time I went to my closet, I found a pair of pants with a price tag on them. I remembered how long I had shopped for those pants knowing that I had a blouse that needed the perfect pants to wear it with. Those pants were perfect for that purpose, but I never wear long, hot pants here on the island, so it was a foolish purchase. Now I am mindful of each purchase I make. My criteria is: *do I love it, do I need it, do I feel beautiful in it, and would I wear it?* If I can't answer yes to all those questions, I don't buy it.

When I met Ron, one of the first things he showed me was his closet. Wow! I had never seen a bigger, more beautiful, meticulous closet. He had many suits, shirts, ties and so many shoes! I could imagine the life he had been living, but I knew it didn't reflect his life currently. As we got to know each other, we talked about the closet, and he decided it was time for him to release the clothes he did not need and wouldn't be wearing again. He made a lot of people happy! But those shoes were a challenge for him. I knew that they were high-quality shoes and were worth a fortune, but I didn't know they were all a gift from his friend Nirvana. His friend loved shoes and didn't resist buying any that struck his fancy, so after he wore them once or twice, he passed them on to Ron and his other friends. Fortunately for Ron, they wore the same size. Eventually, Ron discovered one of his friends wore the same size, so his friend got to enjoy the collection. I am grateful that Ron cleaned out his closet then so that we didn't have to bring all those clothes and shoes to Maui and more so that I didn't have to deal with all that when he was gone. And he made many people happy with his gifts!

Think of the joy you will be bringing people as you clean out your closet. Take the time to ask yourself...*do I love it, do I need it, do I feel beautiful in it, and would I wear it?* What we wear says so much about ourselves. When you wear something you love, that you feel beautiful in, your mood and your actions will broadcast that beauty and love. And it doesn't even matter who sees you. That beauty and love can bounce right back at you from your mirror. Even if you are home working in the garden, put on something that reflects your joy. Instead of baggy sweats and a T-shirt, wear comfortable shorts and a bright top, and you will feel better. Try it! Of course, there is always a place for those comfy sweats when you cuddle up with a bowl of popcorn to watch a good movie, so don't toss things from your closet willy-nilly. Choose to keep what makes you smile and feel good.

Try releasing the items of clothing you never wear. Clean out your closet for items that are out of date. The Salvation Army or the women's shelter will love you for donating those items to them. You will love the new space you have created. Clothes can trigger memories, so release the ones you don't want to remember and shop for new memories you want to make. Find clothes that make you feel good, and release clothes that don't. Have fun!

PRACTICE: CLEAN YOUR CLOSET

Cleaning out your closet is a great way to release clothing you no longer need or want. Start by getting three big plastic bags: One trash, one donate, and one garage sale or consignment store. I don't use that third bag because I prefer to pay things forward, but if you like to have sales or do consignment shops, by all means, have fun. Sort things thoughtfully. You don't want any regrets from the process. When you run across something you aren't sure about, set it aside. You can always come back to it later.

As you do the process, don't forget your shoes or anything else you have stored in your closet. Empty out your closet as you go, and sort. When it is empty, take a good look at it. *Is there a way you could rearrange it so that it would serve you better? Could you use a shoe rack or laundry hamper? Maybe you would like to give it a good cleaning and maybe even a coat of paint.* Since you are the primary audience for your closet, you could paint it any way you like. Or, you may paint a picture, maybe a landscape or an abstract. Whatever you choose, it should make you smile when you open the doors to your closet.

You may want to get a set of nice flat hangers with a coating that keeps your clothes from falling off. With the flat hangers, you can fit more things in your closet, and they are inexpensive if you shop at the right places! When you get your closet all neat and orderly, plan to keep it that way. Having a sense of order can bring your peace. And while you are at it, you may want to clean out your dresser drawers. Be sure to take care of those bags you filled. Throw out the trash and deliver the others where they need to go.

Now don't you feel lighter? Clearing out your closet can do much to boost your mood and keep you going in a positive direction.

Key Tips for Chapter Twenty-Five

* Let go of the items in your closet you no longer enjoy.
* Others can benefit from our generosity.
* Releasing excess allows us room to evolve.

Take Action

HAPPINESS HABITS

Your Intention

* Write an *Intention* about when and what you are going to clean out your closet and dresser drawers.

I intend to _____

_____

_____

_____

Your Gratitude

 * Write what you are *grateful* about for the things you choose to save.
   I am happy and grateful that _____

_____

_____

_____

_____

Your Happiness

 * Of all the items you released from your closet, what three things made
   you happiest to let go, and *why did releasing them make you happy?*

_____

_____

_____

_____

Your Affirmation

 * Write a *positive affirmation* about how, moving forward, you will
   change the wardrobe you purchase.
   I am _____

_____

_____

_____

_____

_____

_____

CHAPTER 26

BE OPEN TO LOVE

"What you are seeking is seeking you."
−REV. CHERYL WARD

Elisabeth Kübler-Ross, famed psychiatrist and death and dying expert, is quoted as saying that "there are essentially only two human emotions, love and fear."[9] When a loved one passes, the depth of our love, challenged by the height of our fear, can throw us into a state of uncertainty. We can know in our hearts that love goes on forever, but when our loved one is no longer there, we often fear that we can't or don't want to live without love. This dichotomy is the basis of grief. When we accept that we can love still and again, we begin to release the fear.

The death of a loved one changes everything. Adjusting to the grief experience takes time, depending on the relationship you had. By evaluating the importance of love in your life, you can discover the multiplicity of its sources. You still love the person who passed and will most likely love that person for the rest of your life, even if they aren't with you. For instance, I love both of my husbands, my parents, my sister, and countless relatives and friends, even though they passed. I also love those still with me, like my children and dear

---

[9] https://www.skilledatlife.com/why-we-need-to-know-that-all-emotions-stem-from-either-love-or-fear/#:~:text=Search%20Main%20menu-,Why%20We%20Need%20to%20Know%20That%20All%20Emotions%20Stem%20from,emotions%20stem%20from%20these%20two

friends. When I think about that, I realize I have been building up a plethora of love from many sources, which always brings me comfort.

On the other hand, when a loved one passes, we often feel alone, which brings fear. We sense a lack of companionship and safety that can become overwhelming if we allow it to. When we start to fall into that dark place, it is time to contemplate what we want. What came to me at that time was that I wanted to love and be loved. To me, that was more important than anything. When I thought about it, though, I realized I still have many people to love in my life and many people who love me. That helped me realize I am always open to love. Being open to love, whenever and however it comes, allows you to not second guess, to not say it's too soon or too late. Be open to love and its important place in your life. Knowing everything is perfect will allow love to find you when the time is right.

When Is It Time to Consider Romantic Love?

There will come a time when people ask you if you are ready to start dating. Chances are they are simply conversing, but they may also see something in you that shows them it's time. Be prepared for comments like, *"Don't you think it's too soon for you to date again?"* or *"Isn't it time you met someone?"*. People will say this out of concern for you, not wanting you to be lonely. At first, it may feel unwanted or even scary. Yet, over time or when the time is right, you will know you are ready to welcome love into your life. Allow it to unfold naturally. Start by welcoming friends into your life first and see what happens from there.

As soon as you start dating, trust your choices, feelings, and inner knowingness. Your family may never be ready for you to meet someone new, so commit to doing what you know is best for you, and don't worry about what anyone else thinks. Love is not something we can contain or hold ourselves back from. Your love is not controlled by what others think. Many people will feel you are ready and others will not. You must decide for yourself with the belief in your heart that love is possible for you.

Often when your relationship is deep and seemingly perfect, you can't imagine being with anyone else. Also, the thought of solitude can be terrifying when you have not lived alone. In these circumstances, it is easy to jump into a relationship when you aren't right for each other. On the other hand, you may not be able to imagine being able to get close to someone new, especially physically. You might start thinking things like *how it would feel to be naked with someone again,* and that might stop you cold. You may feel that you have somehow lost your self-confidence. Even when you know that you don't want to be alone, you need a better excuse than that to find someone new.

How will you know when you are ready to date again? Know that there is no ideal timeline. You are ready when you are ready, no matter what anyone else thinks. Start by making a list of the qualities you would like in someone you would consider dating. What is most important to you? For instance, thinking that most people have the same values that you do can be naive. If you value honesty and you discover someone you are interested in lacks integrity, you will know that person is not the one. Start by listing important qualities first. Then go on to make a list of who your ideal partner would be. Being prepared by knowing the qualities you are looking for will save you the experience of going out with someone who doesn't have relationship potential.

DEFINING LOVE FOR YOU

When you write the qualities you desire, which I suggest you do, you will know in your heart who would be your potential successful partner. When you get your heart set on the most important qualities you are sure of, the next step is to get out there. Chances are, your new love won't come knocking on your door. Your friends may have some ideas for you and be willing to set you up, but they may not be looking for what you are. Share with them the kind of partner you desire to attract. Let them know your preferences and your non-negotiables.

Another way to discover someone interesting is to go where you think they would go. If you like plays or concerts, go there. If you like sports, go to games or join a team. If you like to be physically fit, join a gym, enter competitions, or hang out at the juice bar that athletes frequent. Consider doing some community service in an area you are passionate about. You might find a like-minded person there.

When you start falling in love, you may feel conflicted, wondering how you could possibly love two people simultaneously, but the good news is, you can. There will always be a special place in your heart for your loved one who died. You may feel that you can never love again as you did before, and you may not. But you can learn to love again in a new way. And, you may suffer from fear which may be deep, and demonstrate it in the form of a physical reaction or emotional response. Always be gentle with yourself. Having a friend you can share what's happening with can be invaluable.

NEW RELATIONSHIPS

When you do date, only date people up to your standards. Don't compromise. If you notice that a person isn't kind or honest, you don't want to be with them. The person must recognize your worth as you see theirs. Even if you are on your first date, if you can't see yourself growing old with the person, do both of you a favor and don't go out together again.

Realize that your new relationship will never be the same as your old relationship, and that's a good thing. A new relationship will bring you new experiences, love, and a whole new world. Enjoy your discoveries while not focusing on how life used to be. Live right where you are in the moment and live full out with all the joy and energy you can muster. Connect with your love for your new self and enjoy the new love you can create.

In these new experiences that are happening, don't get lost. You can still have the friends and family you had before, even though you are discovering new ones. Stay in touch. Honor and respect your relationships. Be sure to do some things apart, like having lunch with a friend or going to do your favorite things. Pursue interests important to you that you may not share. Take good care of you.

Take your time. There is no rush. Know what you want and what you don't. *Are you ready to move ahead? Are you ready to give up or share material possessions, especially the ones you shared with your loved one who died? Are you ready to share your spiritual life with someone? Are you ready to incorporate someone else's family and friends into your life and your family and friends into their life? Do you feel like you are giving up anything you cherish? Do you feel like you are gaining more in your life? Do you feel like you are settling for less than you desire? Do you see the potential for more than you have dreamed of? Do you love the person you are with a new person in your life?* When you are comfortable with your answers to all these questions, be brave and move forward.

"There are only two days in the year that nothing can be done. One is called yesterday and the other is called tomorrow, so today is the right day to love, believe, do, and mostly live."
–The Dalai Lama

PRACTICE: QUALITIES OF LOVE

You may or may not ever desire to be with someone else romantically, and that's okay. But know that you can be in loving relationships with people for the rest of your life. Make a list of the qualities about your loved one that you most cherish, then add to that list the qualities of any new friend or relationship you would like to have. You will discover that some qualities are of paramount importance to you, while others don't really concern you. Now whenever you meet someone new for any kind of relationship, mentally go through your list of qualities and be sure the new person is one you can comfortably spend time with. Most importantly, enjoy the new people you meet.

KEY TIPS FOR CHAPTER TWENTY-SIX

* Finding new friends is good.
* Know the qualities of the people you most want to be around.
* You can love again if you want to.

TAKE ACTION

HAPPINESS HABITS

Your Intention

* Write an *Intention* about moving forward in your life from now.

I intend to _____

_____

_____

_____

_____

Your Gratitude

* Write what you are *grateful* for in the relationship you have with your loved one who died.

I am happy and grateful that _____

_____

_____

_____

_____

_____

_____

_____

Your Happiness

* In relation to what you read in Chapter 26 about your grief timeline, *what are you anticipating will bring you happiness as you move forward in dealing with your grief?*

_____

_____

_____

_____

_____

Your Affirmation

* Write a *positive affirmation* about what you are changing in your life as you move forward.

I am _____

_____

_____

_____

_____

_____

Chapter 27
Moving Through

My hope is that as we come to the end of this book, you are feeling better. I imagine that many of the chapters were at times challenging, yet I believe over time they were able to help and support you through your grieving process. How you felt when you began and how you feel now is a combination of being open to learning new things and trying them out in your life. You have taken a huge step forward by reading and using this book. The skills you have obtained will support you in having more happiness in your life.

Grief is a process we all go through when we have lost someone we love. How we move through that with grace and ease takes time and effort. I trust that since you have made it to the end of this book, you have found more peace and a deeper sense of well-being through all that you have learned.

As you move forward with your life, I wish only the best for you and that you discover your new purpose in life, as everything is different for you now.

If you would like to know more about how you can find happiness and joy while grieving, I invite you to visit my website at www.griefandhappiness. com—I also do one-on-one sessions where we can go deeper, and I can assist you in moving forward. If you like to contact me for more information, you can always do so. I also have a Facebook page called *The Grief and Happiness Alliance*, and teach classes online where I show you how to ease the pain of grieving through journal writing. Go to www.griefandhappiness.com

I am proud to be the founder of the *Grief and Happiness Alliance*, which meets every week online to write together, discuss what we write, learn happiness practices, and make new friends. I invite you to join us any time. *The Grief and Happiness Alliance Nonprofit Organization* offers special events and classes and provides funding for such activities so that there is no charge to those attending.

With the support of our nonprofit organization, I have also produced a Grief and Happiness card deck to help you find comfort. The deck of fifty-two cards is designed to support you for a year by. pulling out a card every week to read and contemplate. Each lovely card also has a different picture of the beauty of Maui, Hawaii to enjoy. This beautiful box of cards also makes a perfect gift. If you'd like to know more or order a set for yourself or a friend, go to https:// www.griefandhappiness.com/ where you can also order a beautifully designed copy of this book. All the profits from the sale of this book and the cards go to *The Grief and Happiness Alliance Nonprofit Organization* to fund their services for people who are dealing with grief and loss.

As you continue on in your grieving, know that joy and happiness are always available to you when you are ready, and if this book has helped you find a tiny bit more of it, then I am happy. I have done my job. My greatest wish is for those that are experiencing the sorrow of grief to find comfort and support. I want all people who are hurting to know that you can find happiness at the same time. I hope this book has helped you do just that.

By reading *The Grief and Happiness Handbook*, you have learned many tools which will help you to take the best care of yourself while grieving and discovering your beautiful new life. Take all the time you want to, and enjoy all the new friends you make along the way. The actions you take from this moment on allow you to thrive by embracing happiness, being kind, letting go of fear, forgiving everything you need to, and expressing gratitude. Know that grieving and being happy at the same time is natural and ideal. You can have both and be in harmony with each of those feelings as you move forward and become the happy person you are meant to be.

May all your days be special and your thoughts be filled with love.

Much love and care,
Emily

Additional Information

About the Grief and Happiness Alliance

The Grief and Happiness Alliance is a safe space where the group provides a place for people dealing with loss to come together on a regular basis where they can find comfort, support, love, and happiness. At each meeting, we write about grief, learn happiness practices, and make new friends. People attend from all over the world. We invite you to join us at no charge. Find out more at https://www.griefandhappiness.com/

About the Grief and Happiness Alliance Nonprofit Organization

The Grief and Happiness Alliance Nonprofit Organization was formed by a group of compassionate supporters who see the value and necessity of loving and providing resources for those dealing with grief and loss. We are open to new members who share our vision. The organization is supported by donations to ensure that our resources are available at no charge to those who would love this support.

The Grief and Happiness Alliance Nonprofit Organization published this book, The Grief and Happiness Handbook: Taking Action to Thrive Through Grief, and The Grief and Happiness Cards: Gentle Support for Dealing with Grief and Finding Happiness to help raise funds to ensure the activities of the organization continue to thrive in support of our Purpose, Mission, Vision,

Mission, and Core Values. We exist because of your generosity and are grateful for your support.

https://www.griefandhappiness.com/the-grief-and-happiness-nonprofit-organization-info

* **Our Purpose**
    * Our purpose is to provide comfort and emotional support to those dealing with the many expressions of grief and loss. Members will discover a supportive community and learn skills to recapture the experience of happiness.
* **Vision**
    * Our vision is to create and sustain a supportive presence that provides a variety of resources addressing the needs of those dealing with grief and loss.
* **Mission**
    * Our mission is to serve people dealing with grief and loss by providing online gatherings, building community, and offering workshops and retreats that teach skills for reclaiming happiness.
* **Core Values**
    * Compassion
    * Integrity
    * Optimism
    * Philanthropy
    * Respect
    * Joy
    * Inclusion

In Gratitude

So many people contributed to the fruition of *The Grief and Happiness Handbook*. The inspiration was provided by those who have been on the journey of living, transitioning, and loving me through it all. My husbands Rev. Ron Threatt and Jacques Thiroux valiantly lived every moment to the fullest. Yvonne Demetriff, Shena Medley, and Robin Garrison loved and supported me on the way. Lori and Chap Morris for their love and inspiration.

I am eternally grateful to many friends who contributed their experiences: Karen Brown, Patti Ross, Marla Iyasere, Ellis Wynne, Kayrn Shaudis, Nancy Edelhertz, Brooke Brown, Maryann Michalski Cord, Annis Cassells, Lynel Johnson, Saundy Sparling, Cathy Butler, Carla Stanley, Bonnie Neubauer, Rev. Rachel Hollander, Julie Sherwood Bumatay, Kelly Maple, Bambi Poindexter, and Jeanette Richardson Herring. Many other friends and family inspired and supported me: Fontaine and Mike Huey, Rose and Sophie Rabinov, Willie and Michelle Davis, Linda Robinson, Stephen Thiroux, Jennifer Adrian, Katie Thiroux, Matt Witek, Rickie Byars, Rev. Greta Sesheta, Rev. Deborah Johnson, Rev. Michael Bernard Beckwith, Saffronia Threatt, Yusef Alexandrine, Anhthu Li, Dawn Wade, Henry Blenner, Maggie Hood, Jason Thiroux, Abigale Auffant, Sharon Toutant, Ryn Kapahulehua, Kimokea, Adisina Ogunelese, Adrian Antonescu, Alexis Witek, Bodhi Be, Christine Burke, Debbie Adams. Guinevere PH Dethlefson, Mila Poaipuni, Isabel Thrioux, Gina Satriano, Jeanette Hablewitz, Jeff Zimmerman, Joe Petersen, Justin Kauflin, Orville and Hazel Lofton, Pam Galbraith, Ron and Julie Metoyer, Sydney Thiroux, Shea Derrik, Kevin Kastle, Shirley Brewer, and Tom Faught.

Finally, I give thanks to the *Grief and Happiness Alliance Nonprofit Organization* (GHANO) for their support in publishing *The Grief and Happiness Handbook*. The Core Values of the GHANO include compassion, respect, optimism, inclusion, and Joy. These values and the mission of serving people dealing with grief and loss are brought to light in this handbook. GHANO also provides online gatherings and workshops, building community for our purpose.

Learn more at https://www.griefandhappiness.com/ and register each week for our meeting, which is at no charge to you, here: https://www.griefandhappiness.com/the-grief-and-happiness-nonprofit-organization

My intention in writing *The Grief and Happiness Handbook* is to provide love and support to anyone who is navigating a journey of grief.

ABOUT THE AUTHOR

Emily Thiroux Threatt is a lecturer, author, and speaker with extensive personal experience in the grieving process due to the deaths of her two husbands, as well as her Father, Mother, Aunts, Uncles, and many friends. She has learned to face life with love, optimism, and joy. In turn, she has created a unique program called, "Writing Your Way Through Grief" to help others through the grieving process.

She holds a master's degree in English with a concentration in Writing. She has been teaching writing and composition at college and university levels for over 30 years. During that time, she wrote three writing textbooks, published by Prentice Hall™ and Pearson Education™.

She participated with the Bereaved Person's Association in Bakersfield, California, which her husband Jacques Thiroux co-founded. She also assisted her bioethicist husband with multiple revisions of his popular text, "Ethics: Theory and Practice," published by Prentice Hall and Pearson Education.

Emily conducts workshops, speaking engagements, and retreats on transforming from loss to joy on the mainland of the United States and in her home in Maui, Hawaii.

To learn more, please visit her website at: https://lovingandlivingyourway throughgrief.com/

Author Bio

Emily Thiroux Threatt is the author of the books *The Grief and Happiness Handbook: Taking Action to Thrive Through Grief* and *Loving and Living Your Way Through Grief: A Comprehensive Guide to Reclaiming and Cultivating Joy and Carrying on in the Face of Loss* and has shared her story in the international bestselling compilation book, *Ignite Forgiveness.* She is also the creator of *The Grief and Happiness Cards: Gentle Support for Dealing With Grief and Finding Happiness.*

In addition to writing her books to provide comfort and support to people dealing with grief and loss, Emily founded the *Grief and Happiness Alliance,* a free weekly meeting that happens virtually to support those who are grieving. Members write together and do happiness practices to move through the grieving process with greater peace and ease. She founded *The Grief and Happiness Alliance Nonprofit Organization* to fund those meetings and provide other services for those who are grieving.

Emily is also the host of the ongoing *Grief and Happiness* weekly podcast, which has over 100 episodes currently. She is a *Happy For No Reason*™ certified trainer. She is also a retired university lecturer in writing and has written three college textbooks.

For most of her life, Emily has used journal writing to express her emotions. After her second husband died, she naturally turned to writing to help deal with her grief. Emily then discovered she could also use writing to help friends deal with grief. This led her to a career of teaching and writing books about the power of writing to move through the grieving process.

Emily retired on the beautiful island of Maui after a rich and varied career in owning and operating businesses ranging from an ambulance company to a live theater, a school of arts, an art gallery, and a cafe and a catering company. Her passions are ceramics, acting, directing, designing, weaving, quilting, and cooking, and she is a certified vegan chef.

Emily has journeyed through grief multiple times, and despite losing her two husbands, she has learned to face life with love, optimism, and joy. She aims to comfort and support those dealing with grief and loss by teaching them how to focus on happiness. She deeply believes that joy, happiness, and grief can exist together and that a new love for life will emerge through understanding grief.

OTHER BOOKS BY THE AUTHOR

Loving and Living Your Way Through Grief: A Comprehensive Guide to Reclaiming and Cultivating Joy and Carrying on in the Face of Loss January 19, 2021

Ignite Forgiveness: A Journey in Forgiveness, Peace, and Inner Harmony by JB Owen, Tish Meehan, Emily Thiroux Threatt. November 2, 2022

The Critical Edge: Thinking and Researching in a Virtual Society 1999

Cultures: Diversity in Reading and Writing 1st Edition, 1993 2nd Edition 1997

Resources

The Grief and Happiness Alliance and Nonprofit Organization

https://www.griefandhappiness.com/

Grief and Happiness Newsletter

http://eepurl.com/gO48Kn

Loving and Living Your Way Through Grief

https://lovingandlivingyourwaythroughgrief.com

Grief and Happiness podcast

https://podcasts.apple.com/us/podcast/grief-happiness/id1589284828

Instagram

https://www.instagram.com/emily_thiroux_threatt/

LinkedIn

https://www.linkedin.com/in/emily-thiroux-threatt/

Twitter

https://twitter.com/ThreattEmily

Facebook

https://www.facebook.com/groups/546850166524931

TRADEMARKS

HEIFER INTERNATIONAL'S SEEDS OF CHANGE INITIATIVE is a **trademark** of Heifer Project International.

MADD is a **trademark of Mothers Against Drunk Driving.**

UNITEDHEALTH GROUP INTERNATIONAL is a **trademark** of **UnitedHealth Group** Incorporated.

ALOHATUDE is a **trademark** of **Ululani's** Hawaiian Shave Ice, LLC.

POOR LITTLE RICH GIRL is a **trademark** of La Jolla Group, Inc

YOUTUBE Trademark of GOOGLE LLC

DRESS FOR SUCCESS is a trademark and brand of Dress for Success Worldwide

ZOOM is a **trademark** of **Zoom** Video Communications, Inc

GOFUNDME is a **trademark** of **GoFundMe** Inc.

PANDORA is a **trademark** of **Pandora** Jewelry, LLC.

THE CROWN is a **trademark** of Lee & G Associates Inc.

CALL THE MIDWIFE is a **trademark** of Neal Street Productions Limited.

GREY'S ANATOMY is a **trademark** of Disney Enterprises, Inc..

TED LASSO is a **trademark** owned by Warner Bros. Entertainment Inc.

ONLY MURDERS IN THE BUILDING is a **trademark** of Twentieth Century Fox Film Corporation

FACEBOOK is a **trademark** owned by **Facebook**, Inc

MEETUP is a **trademark** of **MEETUP** LLC.

GOOGLE is a trademark of **GOOGLE INC**

THE NOTEBOOK is a **trademark** of E*TRADE FINANCIAL HOLDINGS, LLC.

WORD is a trademark of MICROSOFT CORPORATION.

RESTORE is a trademark of Habitat for Humanity International, Inc..

BOYS & GIRLS CLUBS is a trademark of BOYS AND GIRLS CLUBS OF AMERICA, INC.

UHG is a trademark of UNITEDHEALTH GROUP INCORPORATED.

SPOTIFY is a trademark of Spotify AB.

Amazon and all related Marks are Trademarks of Amazon.com, Inc. or its affiliates

ITUNES is a trademark of Apple Inc.

PRENTICE-HALL is a trademark of SAVVAS LEARNING COMPANY LLC.

PEARSON is a trademark of Pearson plc.

HALLMARK is a trademark of HALLMARK LICENSING LLC.

Printed in Great Britain
by Amazon

45744163R00175